Meditate the Tantric Yoga Way

Dedicated to

GURUDEV

Paramhansa Swami Satyananda Saraswati

Meditate the Tantric Yoga Way

by Swami Jyotirmayananda Saraswati
translated and edited by Lilian K. Donat

London. George Allen & Unwin Ltd Ruskin House Museum Street

First published in 1973

ISBN 0 04 149022 3 hardback
0 04 149023 1 paperback

Printed in Great Britain
in 12 point Baskerville type
by Unwin Brothers Limited
Woking and London

Contents

* These chapters should be practised listening to the voice of the teacher, a tape or a record.

Glossary

AJNA	Command, also the name of cakra inside the head at the level of the centre between the eyebrows
AKASHA	Ether, space
ANAHATA	Immortal, also the name of cakra in the region of the heart
ANTAR	Inner
ANUSHTANA	Great undertaking
ASANA	Posture
ATMAN	Soul
BIJA	Seed
BIJA MANTRA	Mantra which consists of the root of a word
BINDU	Point, dot, also the name of cakra at the back of the head
BHRUMADYA	Centre between the eyebrows, important for concentration and meditation
CAKRA (pronounced chakra)	Plexus. There are many cakras in the body. The most important ones are concentrated and meditated upon
CAKRA VEDHANA	Piercing of the cakras
CHANDA	Smell
CHAYA	Shadow
CIDAKASA (pronounced Chidakasha)	Experience of infinite space within and without

CIT	Consciousness
DHARANA	Deep concentration
DHYANA	Meditation
DIKSHA	Initiation, consecration
GARBHA	Womb
GERU	Soft ochre-coloured stone used for dying robes. Also the name of a colour
GURU	One who dispels darkness
HARE, HARI	One of the names of Vishnu
HARI OM TAT SAT	God is, that is the truth. This is used as Mantra and also as greeting
HIRANYA	Golden
HIRANYA GARBHA	Literally, golden womb; meaning cosmic consciousness from which the concept of God (Isvara) evolves as the trinity of Brahma (creator), Vishnu (preserver) and Shiva (one who dissolves)
IDA	Psychic nerve current flowing through the left nostril down to the left of the spinal cord
ISHTA DEVATA	Favourite deity
JAPA	Repetition
JIVA	Individual
KARMA	Action, seed of action
KARMENDRIYA	Organ of action

KOSA (pronounced kosha)	Sheath or covering of soul
KSHATRIYA	Warrior caste
KUNDALINI	Serpent power. Primordial cosmic energy which lies, coiled up, in Muladhara cakra
MADHYAMA	Middle, refers to a sound between two tones, one audible and one inaudible
MAHA	Great, supreme
MAHAYOGIN	Supreme yogi
MAITHUNA	Intercourse
MALA	Kind of rosary, usually with 108 beads
MANASIKA	Mental repetition of Mantra
MANDUKI	Female frog, also one of the postures
MANIPURA	Literally abode of jewel, also the name of cakra on level with the navel
MANTRA	Mystical syllable or syllables for spiritual communion
MAUNA	Silence
MERU	Centre bead of mala which must not be crossed
MULADHARA	Root, foundation, also name of the lowest cakra in the body
MULABANDHA	Contraction of the anus sphincter
NADA	Sound
NAMA	Name
NASIKAGRA	Tip of the nose
NASIKA DRISTI	Gaze at the tip of the nose
NAVA MUKI	Nine openings (of the body)
NIDRA	Sleep

NIYAMA	Observance of law, regulation
OM	Sacred syllable symbolizing God
PADA	Foot
PADMA	Lotus
PADMASANA	Lotus posture
PARA	Beyond, transcendental
PINGALA	Psychic nerve current flowing through the right nostril down to the right of the spinal cord
PRANA	Life-force
PRANAYAMA	Breathing exercises, breath control
PRASADA	Offering of food to God
PRATYAHARA	Withdrawal of senses from objects
PRATYAYA	Cause, mental effort
RAGA	Form of classical music
RASA	Taste
RISHI	Seer
RUDRAKSHA	A fruit, the seeds of which are used for malas
RUPA	Form, sight
SHABDA	Sound
SAHASRARA	Thousand-petalled lotus, also the name of the cakra inside the crown of the head
SAMADHI	Superconscious state
SAMSKARAS	Innate impressions
SANKALPA	Resolve
SANYASIN	A renunciate, monk
SHAKTI	Cosmic energy, power

SHANTI	Peace
SHASTRA	Scripture
SHIVA LINGA	Symbol of Shiva, usually represented by an egg-shaped stone
SIDDHI	Psychic power
SPARSA	Touch
SUSHUMNA	Central nerve channel between Ida and Pingala
SVADHISHTHANA	Standing by oneself, also name of a cakra
SWAMI	Master, spiritual teacher
TANTRA	Particular path of Yoga with worship of goddess or shakti
TRATAKA	Steady gazing
TULASI	Sacred plant of India belonging to the basil family
UJJAYI	Breathing exercise, also used in meditation
UPAMSU	Humming, whispering
UPASANA	Literally, sitting near, worship
VAIKHARI	Tone produced by humming or whispering
VAJRASANA	Thunderbolt posture
VEDAS	The most ancient authentic Indian scriptures
VIDYA	Knowledge
VISHUDDHI	Purified, also the name of cakra
YAMA	Restraint, also name of the Lord of Death
YANTRA	Geometrical form used for meditation
YOGA	Union, to join, to fuse
YOGA MUDRA	Yogic posture
YOGA NIDRA	The sleep of the yogi, relaxation and meditation technique
YOGI	One who practises yoga

Introduction

The word 'Yoga', derived from the verbal root 'yuj', has many meanings. One of them is to assume a yoke, another one is union and yet another one means to join, but in the sense of fusing. People who practise Yoga often consider themselves to be Yogis; but to perform Asanas and even to sit in a trance-like state in meditation, does not mean that one has become a Yogi. The true Yogi detaches himself from everyday life, not by escaping from it but by trying to reach autonomy and so finding his inner freedom.

Various paths with many techniques lead towards this goal. The best known are the four main branches of Yoga.

Karma-Yoga, the path of work and service,
Bhakti-Yoga, the path of loving devotion,
Jnana-Yoga, the path of knowledge,
Hatha-Yoga and its continuation, Raja-Yoga, the path of bodily integration and mastery of oneself through certain psychophysical methods.

These four paths correspond with the four functions of man: to sense, to feel, to think and to will. The grouping of the functions varies from person to person. What is the less dominant function in one will be the leading function in another. Everybody has two leading functions; the third is unconscious and the fourth is less dominant.

Problems usually arise out of the fourth (the less dominant) function which explodes the unity of a person, splitting it into many facets. Besides this, man moves alternatively through the various realms of consciousness: waking, dreaming, sleeping and thinking. (See diagram.)

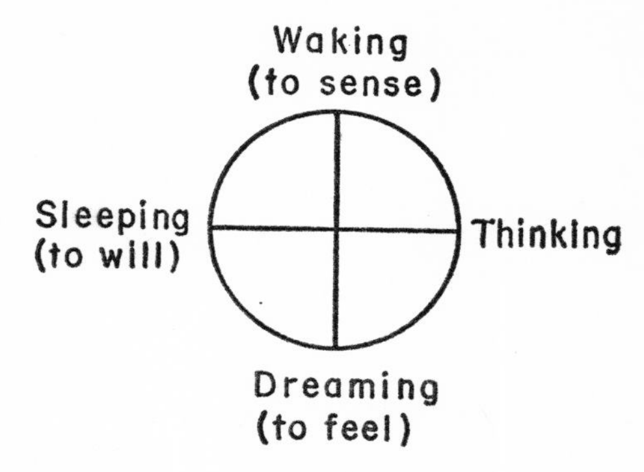

Awake, he identifies himself with his reactions to his environment and with thoughts which he believes to be his own creation. During deep sleep he is practically unconscious and in dream sleep his subconscious predominates.

Union, as the aim of Yoga, means the experience of wholeness. It also means the unity of the four functions in the various realms of consciousness. The goal has only been reached when one becomes a continuous, detached witness of one's own personality even while dreaming and sleeping. It is comparatively simple to observe oneself while being awake, the way one acts and reacts, speaks, moves, etc., but it becomes considerably more difficult during the process of thinking; while dreaming, it is sometimes possible to be conscious that one dreams; while sleeping, this knowledge would mean perfection.

We have to penetrate from mere 'awarenesses' into consciousness itself. This consciousness is nothing other than the witness whose presence can be experienced in the background. This witness is always the same—whether we are ten, twenty or sixty years old. It is called the 'I'.

If this 'I' is experienced as a unity, that is in harmony with the four functions and with the constant flux of the 'awarenesses' (Pratyayas), it becomes pure consciousness and is then called the Soul.

The Soul connects the two poles of Body and Spirit and is, as consciousness, the original source, also called life-force. As such it can be experienced as the innermost light inherent in everybody.

Yet everybody is different because each single person consists of three realms, namely Body, Soul and Spirit. Primeval consciousness itself, however, is the same in everybody; it is simultaneously cosmic consciousness and personal integration. (Mathematically expressed, the centre and circumference of an infinite circle are identical.) In Yoga this is called Atman-Brahman.

The three realms of Body, Soul and Spirit together with the four functions (see page oo) form a twelve-fold frame which constitutes the structure of our understanding of the Universe and the Universe itself.

Space and time are fused and it is impossible to separate them. The integration of one's own capacities in the outer world happens when one applies certain spatial qualities at their own, unique moment. If this moment has been missed it is too late. To act in full consciousness according to one's inherent disposition in the world is called 'acting with inner meaning'. When this inner meaning has been experienced life becomes intelligible as purpose and happiness. At the moment of death this inner meaning becomes the vehicle of the soul to enter pure consciousness but if, during life, this meaning has not been understood and man has let himself be driven by his uncontrolled primeval instincts, this consciousness cannot be reached at the moment of death. Space and time will be torn by fearful visions; darkness separates life and death and the personality is annihilated. These last, timeless moments can be referred to as Heaven or Hell.

The path in relation to the world, the experiencing and exhausting of one's personality as a unit and as a definite possibility for both world and history, leads to the goal over the twelve-fold frame. The same integration which takes place on the outer path can also take place on the inner path where 'realms' and 'functions' are experienced in themselves. During meditation time and space are grasped as separate media which have to be brought into harmony. What are those media and where are they located in us? The reply to this question is given in allegorically coded terms in many Yoga texts, particularly in Tantra and Kundalini-Yoga.

Man can take his bearings from one of the two poles which form his personality. One pole is his body, structurized through the chromosomes; the other is the structure of chains of associations in his brain—his unique, particular spirituality—which starts with the first breath drawn by a human being. The choice of the path is left to the individual; he can either be led by his instincts or by his spiritual potentials. To make sense both of these have to be harmonized. Carnality and hedonism are equally the result of uncontrolled manipulation as is undiluted spirituality; the latter is usually accompanied by the suppression of the subconscious and may lead to cold, overbearing intellectuality.

Victory on the threshold of death can only be achieved when the life-force which connects the two poles has been mastered. This mastery is nothing else but the experience of the life-force which, on the inner path, is felt as the witness of consciousness. When both poles have become objectified and appear as an apparent duality in harmony life-force, no longer torn by a tug-of-war, can develop in its original nature and purity. This always happens spontaneously. When, on the one hand, the body as a unit and a field of force, and, on the other hand, the spirit as a constant possibility of development, become objectified and experienced, only then can the illumination by the innermost light take place. Brainwaves no longer radiate outwards but converge to the point-like centre of the brain, when the cosmos becomes both the centre and the frontier of earthly existence. When this last norm has been reached, both spontaneity and pure intuition have been achieved. Life turns into an effortless game and the last freedom becomes the basis of a life in tune with the Universe.

This cosmic consciousness represents pure consciousness in us, the unified essence and totality of the brain, and not a realm which has to be reached step by step. The last state is in us, and nowhere else. No more need to search, suffer, strive and sacrifice or whatever else tradition demands. It is our duty to unveil and objectify what we are. Not more and not less.

Every day we follow a path, though we are not conscious of it. Every night we fall asleep, though not consciously. This daily mechanical functioning of awareness must be brought under control. Here, too, duality is at work: All the material which we absorbed from childhood onwards and the innumerable sense impressions, which, seemingly digested, are deposited in us, form, on the one hand, the basis of our mastery in the world. On the other hand, in their rudimentary form, they turn into waste products, building up Samskaras in our subconscious which bar the way to the light.

In the creation of the world the life-force, Shakti, mostly symbolized as Kali, detaches itself from the eternal, point-like possibility and creates the dual world of name and form, by achieving a constantly increasing density. She comes to rest at the lowest point of cosmic evolution where she forms the potential power of the dissolution of the world. This dissolution must not be confounded with the Last Judgement, but it is a process of consciousness in which man uses this force as a vehicle for rising and reaching the point-like cosmos which is experienced as Samadhi. In Indian art this goal is represented as Maithuna, the union of Shiva and Shakti.

Shakti, resting inside us in the lowest Cakra as potential power, is called Kundalini or the serpent power. The lowest centre called Muladhara-Cakra represents the pole of materiality. The serpent power is also sexual power which, in its most sublimated form, creates a conscious harmony with the highest centre, the Sahasrara-Cakra, which is the seat of supreme consciousness and spirituality.

Between these two centres lie five steps of evolution; these steps, beginning with the highest and moving downwards, symbolize the evolution of the world; those steps which begin at the lowest Cakra and move upwards indicate the evolution of consciousness. Altogether these steps are nothing but the separate elements of space and time. Instead of the numbers 3×4, traditionally symbolized in the Zodiac, we here meet with the numbers $4 + 3$, the seven steps into the light or the number of veils covering the innermost light.

The path between materiality and spirituality, i.e. the wandering along this sevenfold path, happens automatically every day and every night. While this wandering is taking place, the constant changes should be experienced with increasing clarity. The seven paths (or the seven Cakras) are recognized as:

7	Sahasrara SPIRIT	Light	superconscious	SPIRIT
6	Ajna SOUL	between spirit and matter	conscious	SOUL
5	Vishuddhi BODY	Akasha ether	subconscious	BODY
4	Anahata to think	Vayu air	associations	
3	Manipura to will	Agni fire	sleeping	
2	Svadhishthana to feel	Ap water	dreaming	
1	Muladhara to sense	Prithivi earth	waking	

This structure is the key to understanding and only the most important aspects are explained hereafter. The lowest Cakra is the realm of sensing, which, in itself, can be subdivided into five realms:

Chanda (smell)	corresponding with the first Cakra
Sparsha (touch)	corresponding with the second Cakra
Rupa (sight)	corresponding with the third Cakra

7 - SPIRIT					
6 - SOUL	(SHABDA) HEARING	FOOD	CONSEQUENCE	SYNTHESIS	ONENESS
5 - BODY	(RASA) TOUCHING	AGGRESSION	DECISION	ANALYSIS	
4 - THINKING	(RUPA) SEEING	FEAR	DETERMINATION		
3 - WILL	(SPARSA) TASTING	SEX			
2 - FEEL	(CHANDA) SMELLING				
1 - SENSE					

EARTH	=	PRITHIVI	ELEMENTS
WATER	=	AP	
FIRE	=	AGNI	
AIR	=	VAYU	
ETHER	=	AKASHA	

Rasa (taste)	corresponding with the fourth Cakra
Shabda (sound)	corresponding with the fifth Cakra

When all the sense perceptions are experienced in unity, it indicates the prerequisite of the mastery of the waking state, belonging to the first Cakra (Muladhara). (See page 21.) In reality everybody starts at a certain sense organ according to disposition and the limitation of one function or another.

The mastery of the first Cakra uses the first five Cakras as a frame of the five sense perceptions. The first *layer* of every Cakra up to the fifth, which represent the body (see page 22), is dedicated to sensing. The second layer is dedicated to emotion. When the first Cakra has been mastered, the second Cakra can be tackled. The basis for the four emotional instincts is found from the second to the fifth Cakra.

1st instinct in the second Cakra	Sex
2nd instinct on the third Cakra	Fear
3rd instinct in the fourth Cakra	Aggression
4th instinct in the fifth Cakra	Hunger

With the mastery of these instincts the state of dreaming is conquered.

The third layer of the third to the fifth Cakra is dedicated to will. With the mastery of the three aspects: determination (third Cakra), decision (fourth Cakra) and consequence (fifth Cakra) the state of sleeping is mastered.

The fourth layer is dedicated to thinking and with the conquest of the two aspects of analysis (fourth Cakra) and synthesis (fifth Cakra), the state of associations is mastered.

The steps of the Cakras do not lead upwards but inwards. They do not lead into heaven but more and more into solitude. Only when the first aspect, corresponding with the sense perceptions, has been mastered, can the second aspect, corresponding

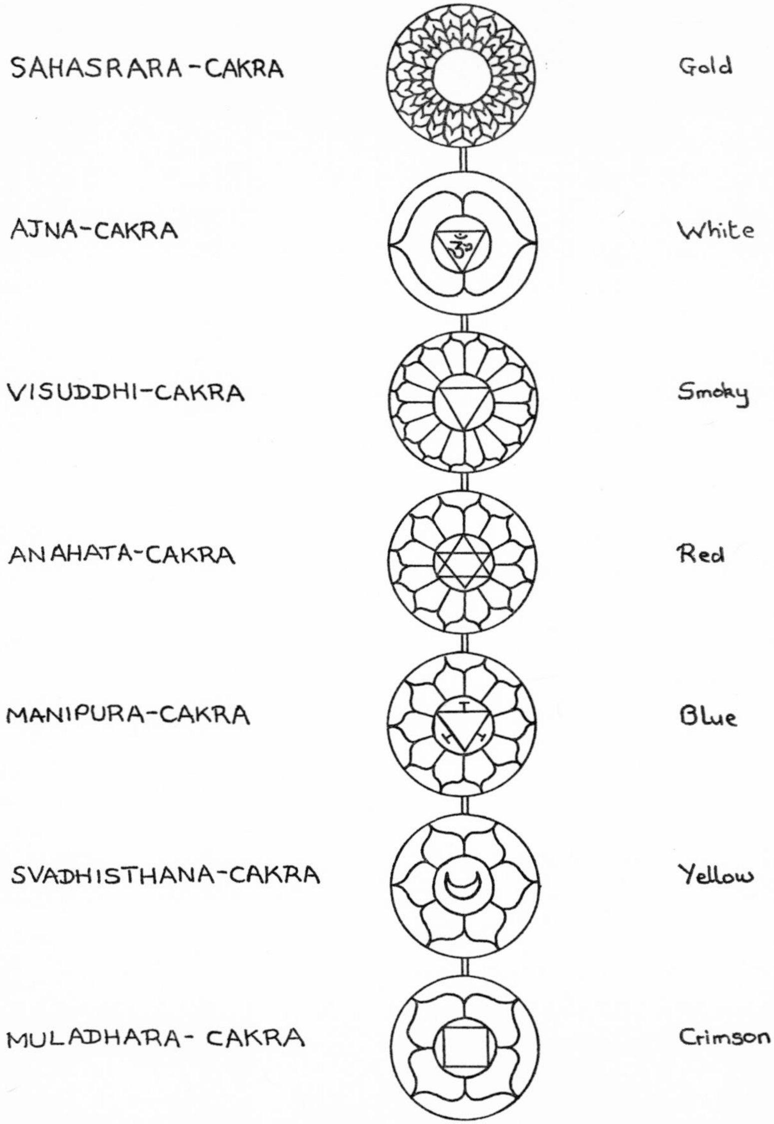

SAHASRARA-CAKRA	Gold
AJNA-CAKRA	White
VISUDDHI-CAKRA	Smoky
ANAHATA-CAKRA	Red
MANIPURA-CAKRA	Blue
SVADHISTHANA-CAKRA	Yellow
MULADHARA-CAKRA	Crimson

with the instincts, be tackled. This means that if I master the first aspect of the fourth Cakra, I have not yet begun to work *on* the fourth Cakra with its corresponding function of thinking, as I am dealing with the fourth step of the first Cakra, namely the sense of touching. In this way the fifth Cakra, the body matter as unity, can be experienced.

The sixth or Ajna-Cakra is placed between matter and spirit. The body or materiality, constituted with the five lower Cakras, forms the connecting material between the two ends of the pole, namely the end of materiality and the end of spirituality. The latter must become objectified through the practice of Karma-Yoga.

Yoga can only lead so far and no further: it does not automatically lead to realization or Samadhi, the mystical union, though it prepares the field. The Rishi Patanjali defines the eight 'limbs' of Yoga as follows:

1. Yama (restraint, moral observance)
2. Niyama (self-discipline, observance of law)
3. Asanas (postures)
4. Pranayama (breathing exercises)
5. Pratyahara (withdrawal of senses from their objects)
6. Dharana (concentration, fixation on object of meditation)
7. Dhyana (deep meditation)
8. Samadhi (superconscious state)

The first two steps are moral codes, demanded in most religions. The third, postures, develops the awareness of the physical body and its unity. The fourth, breathing exercises, has two functions: regulation of the intake of oxygen and instruction in an automatic way of breathing for meditation. The prana or life-force also forms a vehicle of consciousness which is necessary for some forms of meditation where a rotation of consciousness is used.

The first four steps or 'limbs' are self-explanatory. During the fifth, Pratyahara, consciousness is withdrawn from the outer world and only the inner world is experienced.

Dharana, the sixth step, is closely related to the fifth; to prevent precipitation into the unconscious, it is necessary to concentrate on a form or symbol, bringing it into such clear focus that one finally fuses with it. With this the seventh step has been reached. The last step, Samadhi, represents an experience which cannot be described but only circumscribed. When it has been reached, the innermost light illuminates the whole being.

There are no techniques for the last two steps. When deep meditation has been achieved in Dhyana, a state of consciousness without action has taken over.

For most techniques described in this book it is advisable to sit in one of the postures of meditation, preferably Padmasana the Lotus Posture, Vajrasana, the Thunderbolt Posture or one of the others. Should this not be possible, any posture in which spine and head are erect and in which one feels relaxed enough to sit motionless, can be used.

Both worlds, the inner and the outer one, must be mastered simultaneously. The repudiation of the inner world leads to neurosis and manipulations by undiscovered realms in oneself. The repudiation of the outer world leads to hunger and misery. Harmony between East and West is ultimately not a political-sociological-economical problem but one which has to be solved individually by millions of people.

Instructions in the different techniques should be given by a teacher. This applies to those techniques which are marked in the contents. If there is no teacher, a record or tape can be used. Results can only be achieved when the student is taking an active part, i.e. following with complete concentration.

Do not try to do too much at first. What is important is the regularity of practice. Devote about half an hour at least to Asanas and Pranayama and the same time to Meditation. This is best done either in the late evening or in the early morning.

Chapter 1*

Test for the Power of Imagination

In some of the techniques mentioned in this book, particularly in Antar-Mouna, Antar-Trataka but also in Yoga-Nidra (see chapter 7) and Chaya-Upashana (see chapter 6), a certain power of imagination is required. With eyes closed one must visualize something appearing from somewhere out of the dark, or see certain things in picture form. Sometimes this is difficult for the student who does not know how this can take place or just how clearly he ought to see everything. The explanation that the pictures are similar to those in memory, is often no help. At the moment when one tries to remember even the most familiar face, it can happen that parts seem to vanish, everything is blurred or there is a complete blank in the mind. The aim of the following test is to remove this mental block and to create harmony between observation on the one hand and paying attention on the other.

In order to achieve true relaxation it should be practised lying down. If you have difficulties in seeing pictures, simply follow them mentally. After a certain amount of practice the mental block will vanish. The following sentences, sounding as though straight from the classroom, should be practised at the beginning for about two weeks as a preparation for other techniques.

Later on, this test can be repeated when the threshold between Pratyahara and Dharana, mentioned in the Introduction, has been reached. Transition into true meditation is not possible without being able to visualize a form and this test will establish much of the ability required for this transition. It takes approximately one hour. To prevent pain at the back of the head lie on a thin pillow. You must know the symbol for OM, the sign of the cosmic sound, which you can see above the dedication at the beginning of this book. The following method is one of many and it is easy to develop a sequence of pictures corresponding to the particular interests of the student.

When studying the history of art or architecture, for instance, it is often necessary to describe or draw works of art from memory. Good results can also be achieved through the use of sound and there is another technique you can try if you like music. Electronic or concrete music is associative, as the next part of the tune cannot be easily anticipated. This fact is paralleled by the stream of emerging thoughts, pictures or light splinters in us. When listening to sound, these experiences become integrated and after some time the two chains unite, create an unco-ordinated but visible and continuous succession of associations. Listen to the music, sometimes with closed and sometimes with open eyes, sitting or lying down. The only difference consists in the direction of your attention. Try not to listen to the music but watch the reactions formed in yourself. When the pictures cease, open your eyes. The impressions caught with your eyes closed will create further impressions. The hymns by Stockhausen are particularly suitable and effective for some people. The third and fourth regions lead directly to Antar-Mauna and Nada-Yoga (chapters 8 and 9).

TEXT

Close your eyes
Do not move
Relax, be comfortable

Relax, be comfortable
Eyes are closed
Do not move

Look at the inner space, look at Cidakasha, the inner sky, look at the dark inner space, look at Chidakasha, the inner firmament. Imagine a blackboard, a blackboard in a classroom. You see a blackboard in a classroom. You are going to write on this blackboard with white chalk. It is not difficult. I shall tell you what to write.

You will see what you have written on the blackboard in different coloured chalks. Watch and see yourself writing on the blackboard with the chalk in your hand.

Begin Write the numbers as I tell you:

1 comma 2 comma 3 comma 4 comma 5 comma 6 comma
7 comma 8 comma 9 comma 10 full stop

Write with the chalk, do not only imagine it, but really write, follow every stroke and watch how you write and what you write. You see how you are writing on the blackboard with the chalk; be aware. The blackboard Please wipe off everything with the cloth. Take the chalk again and write:

11 comma 12 comma 13 comma 14 comma 15 comma
16 comma 17 comma 18 comma 19 comma 20 full stop

Wipe it off with the cloth and write another line.
First write at the top the following letters D O N O T S L E E P
equals DO NOT SLEEP
In the following line write:

I shall not sleep.

Write very slowly letter by letter.
Erase these two lines.
Prepare yourself to write the numbers again.

21 comma 22 comma 23 comma 24 comma 25 comma
26 comma 27 comma 28 comma 29 comma 30 full stop

Erase with the cloth and look at the blackboard.
Please remember you are writing on the blackboard in this classroom.
You are writing on the blackboard in this classroom.
You are writing with your hands.
You stand in front of the blackboard and begin on the left with a wavy line, a wavy line.
It moves from left to right, from one side to the other.
Now draw a second line under the first, one other wavy line under the first, a wavy line drawn with a chalk on the blackboard.
Erase what you have drawn with the cloth.
Now again the numbers Quite clear and distinctive
Written with the chalk in your hand on the blackboard

31 comma 32 comma 33 comma 34 comma 35 comma
6 comma 36 comma 37 comma 38 comma 40 full stop

Erase with the cloth and take a pink chalk A pink chalk
Write with the pink chalk on the blackboard.

41 exclamation mark 42 exclamation mark 43 exclamation mark
44 exclamation mark 45 exclamation mark 46 exclamation mark
47 exclamation mark 48 exclamation mark 49 exclamation mark
50 full stop

Erase with the cloth and take the pink chalk
Write on the blackboard with the pink chalk
Something very important written with pink chalk

D O N O T S L E E P

Do not sleep   Another line with pink chalk

I D O N O T S L E E P full stop

Read it again what is written in pink chalk: I do not sleep.
Wipe off with the cloth. Look at the blackboard on which you are going to write.
Write with the pink chalk, write on the blackboard in this classroom

51 exclamation mark 52 exclamation mark 53 exclamation mark
54 exclamation mark 55 exclamation mark 56 exclamation mark
57 exclamation mark 58 exclamation mark 59 exclamation mark
60 full stop

Wipe off with the cloth and take a yellow chalk, a yellow chalk.

Nought Nought Nought Please write Nought o o o o o o
New line Write Nought with yellow chalk o o o o o o o
o o

Write new line o o o o

Write new line Please watch the blackboard

with the yellow chalk o o o o o o o o o o

Wipe it all off with the cloth—all lines, the first, second, third, fourth and fifth
all lines

Wipe off all lines with the cloth. Use the white chalk to write on the blackboard. Again with the white chalk make a cross on the board, make a multiplication sign, a cross, a cross, yet another cross, yet another cross, with white chalk make yet another cross, yet another cross, a further cross, yet another cross, new line Yet another cross, a further cross, a further cross, a last cross. With the cloth erase all these lines Take the white chalk Remember the blackboard, see the blackboard clearly within reach, do not forget the white chalk

You write on the blackboard, you write on the blackboard, you write on the blackboard with white chalk

90 comma 89 comma 88 comma 87 comma 86 comma
85 comma 84 comma 83 comma 82 comma 81 full stop
80 comma 79 comma 78 comma 77 comma 76 comma
75 comma 74 comma 73 comma 72 comma 71 full stop

Erase with the cloth Erase with the cloth
White chalk With white chalk draw a line on the blackboard from left to right. Below make another line, then further lines Please continue.
Line after line drawn with that white chalk, from left to right, when one is finished begin the next continue drawing with white chalk straight lines new lines a new line
Erase with the cloth Erase these lines with the cloth
Now draw wavy lines with the white chalk
Erase with the cloth
Take pink chalk and write on the blackboard

o o o o o o o o o o o

New line write with pink chalk: 7 7 7 7 7 7 7 7 7 7

New line
A new line and a full stop Another full stop Another full stop
Yet another full stop Yet another full stop
Yet another full stop Yet another full stop Yet another full stop
New line
With pink chalk draw a star, a star, a star, draw a star, yet another star yet another star yet another star yet another star yet another star
Erase everything with cloth with pink chalk
Write your name on the blackboard, the name in capitals

Erase this Write the symbol for OM, another OM yet another OM yet another OM yet another OM yet another OM New line yet another OM attention yet another OM you write a further OM yet another OM yet another OM yet another OM yet another OM yet another OM yet another OM yet another OM

Erase all lines with the cloth Take the yellow chalk and draw a very large triangle, the base is as wide as the whole blackboard. The lowest line is as wide as the blackboard the triangle reaches to the top, the point touches the top. You draw a beautiful triangle with the yellow chalk, a beautiful triangle. You draw such a large triangle You draw such a large triangle the base as wide as the blackboard
Now draw a triangle standing on its point, the top as wide as the blackboard
Now you see that the triangles cross The apex of each triangle touches the centre of the base of the other. Now erase both Take the white chalk, put away the yellow chalk Draw a triangle the base as wide as the blackboard, With the white chalk draw another triangle with the base as wide as the top of the blackboard

The two triangles cross each other   The apex of each triangle touches the base of the other triangle.
Wipe everything off with the cloth   With white chalk draw vertical lines on the blackboard   as straight as possible
Vertical lines from top to bottom   on the blackboard   Continue, from one side to the other
Draw vertical lines from the top of the blackboard to the bottom
After one line draw the next   The space between the lines is approximately four inches   Please continue
Erase them all, the vertical lines on the blackboard and with white chalk write your name in any way you like it   Your name
Letter by letter   With the white chalk draw the symbol for

OM OM OM OM OM OM OM

New line with white chalk   please be attentive   attentive
Look at the blackboard   Take the white chalk

o comma o comma o comma o comma o comma
o comma o comma New line
o exclamation mark o exclamation mark o exclamation mark
o exclamation mark o exclamation mark o exclamation mark
o exclamation mark o exclamation mark o exclamation mark
o exclamation mark o exclamation mark o exclamation mark

Erase all this   All lines   Attention please
Attention please   Look at the blackboard   Take the white chalk and write clearly,

1 2 3 4 5 6 7 8 9 10 New line 11 write clearly, watch very carefully 12 13 14 15 16 17 18 19 20 New line 21 22 23 24 25 26 27 28 29 30

Erase all this with the cloth Look at the blackboard Put the chalk away Take yellow chalk With the yellow chalk write your name on the blackboard New line

The symbol for OM OM OM OM OM Erase these lines with the cloth Take the pink chalk and draw a small circle

Continue drawing in a circle to form a spiral until the whole blackboard is covered with it

With yellow chalk

Begin with a small inner circle and draw a spiral getting bigger and bigger very slowly and clearly until the whole blackboard is filled with the spirals

Erase everything, erase the spirals with the cloth and take white chalk, white chalk, and draw several small triangles on the blackboard, also some which stand on their apex Draw these small triangles a few more

Erase the triangles with the cloth, erase the triangles with the cloth

Take green chalk, take green chalk and write numbers beginning with 1 and commas between the figures. Count them out yourself, write them down, one after the other, please continue.

The chalk is green, the blackboard is black. You are writing the numbers beginning with figure 1 clearly

Say them out loud beginning with 1 with commas between.

Start a new line when necessary

Please write the numbers on the blackboard with the green chalk

Please write the numbers on the blackboard with the green chalk with commas between the figures Always a new line when necessary.

Erase all lines with the cloth and with white chalk   draw a triangle   With white chalk   Erase it

Take a pink chalk and draw a triangle on the blackboard with very thick strokes. Erase the triangle with the cloth

Take blue chalk, light blue chalk, take blue chalk and draw a triangle on the blackboard with blue chalk   Erase this with the cloth   Take yellow chalk, yellow chalk   And draw a triangle on the blackboard   With yellow chalk draw thick lines   Erase this   And now   take green chalk, green chalk. With green chalk draw a triangle on the blackboard, press the chalk down firmly.

Erase this,   erase it with the cloth. Take dark red chalk and draw a triangle with dark red chalk. Erase this with the cloth and take violet chalk, draw a triangle with violet chalk on the blackboard, press the chalk down firmly.

Erase this and take geru chalk, the colour of Swamis, a glowing saffron chalk orange colour like the sky at dawn.

Take the geru chalk and draw a triangle with geru chalk on the blackboard   Press down firmly.   Erase this with the cloth

Erase this with the cloth.

Draw an exclamation mark, a vertical line with a dot underneath   An exclamation mark with white chalk   Again another exclamation mark with white chalk

Take pink chalk   exclamation mark   exclamation mark   exclamation mark
Take yellow chalk   exclamation mark   exclamation mark   exclamation mark
Take green chalk   exclamation mark   exclamation mark   exclamation mark
Take red chalk   exclamation mark   exclamation mark   exclamation mark
Take blue chalk   exclamation mark   exclamation mark   exclamation mark
Take geru chalk   exclamation mark   exclamation mark   exclamation mark
Take violet chalk   exclamation mark   exclamation mark   exclamation mark

Try to see it all from top to bottom, please look up: white, pink, yellow, green, sorry geru, violet.

Look again at the top and see the first line   white exclamation marks   Second line pink   Third yellow   Fourth green   Fifth red   Sixth blue   Seventh geru   Eighth violet
Once more look up and see the first line, white exclamation mark
Erase all lines with the cloth   Erase all lines with the cloth and quickly take white chalk and draw a straight line.

Draw a yellow straight line   Draw a pink straight line
Draw a yellow straight line   Draw a green straight line
Draw a red straight line   Draw a blue straight line
Draw a geru straight line   Draw a violet straight line
Look at the blackboard   Erase all the straight lines with the cloth.
Take the white chalk and write

o o continue writing steadily with the white chalk
o o When necessary take new line
Write o o o o with white chalk
New line when necessary

(*One minute pause*)

Erase all with the cloth
Erase all lines with the cloth
Wipe your hands and turn away from the blackboard, look here.

HARI OM TAT SAT
HARI OM

Chapter 2

Japa-Yoga

The word 'Japa' means to repeat and in Japa-Yoga a Mantra is being repeated with the help of a Mala, a chain of usually 108 beads, which, superficially, corresponds with the use of a rosary. This method which is easy to learn and yet surprisingly effective, is taught by most Indian Yogis in the West.

Transcendental Meditation, which has been popularized by Maharishi Mahesh Yogi, is nothing but a combination of Manasika-Japa and Antar Mauna. Swami Satchidananda in New York who offers Yoga instead of LSD to his hippy disciples teaches Japa as well as Hatha Yoga.

The Mantra, which can consist of one or more syllables, is given to the disciple by his Guru. It is unnecessary for the layman to understand the science of the Mantra in order to practise it; all that is needed is regularity of habit and the will to persevere. There are various methods of Japa-Yoga.

1. Vaikhari: here the Mantra is pronounced loudly and clearly; longer Mantras are often chanted. One of the best known Mantras, recently produced as a record by the Radha Krishna Temple in London is 'Hare Krishna, Hare Krishna, Krishna, Krishna, Hare Hare. Hare Rama, Hare Rama, Rama Rama, Hare Hare, etc. This Mantra has been chanted in a specially reserved Bhajan Hall for twenty-four hours a day in the Sivananda Ashram in Rishikesh since 1943. There are supposed to be holy places where this Mantra has been chanted for hundreds of years.

2. Upamshu: here the Mantra is hummed or whispered.
3. Manasika: the Mantra is repeated mentally. This technique is explained later on.
4. Likhita: the Mantra is written down in the most meticulous way in a special book; it can be done in red, blue or green ink and has to be repeated several hundred times. The letters should be as small as possible. Sometimes a few hundred of these letters are joined into one big symbol, but usually they are written in lines. During a certain month (Shravana) there is a tradition in the whole of India when Likhita-Japa is practised on leaves of the Bilva tree.

The most frequently used Mantra is 'Om Nama Shivaya'. This is written with a paste made from sandalwood or red powder; the writing is continued during the whole day into the night. The next morning the leaves with their inscriptions are offered to the deity in the temple.

5. Ajapa-Japa: this technique is taught in chapter 10.

For all Japa techniques except Likhita a Mala is necessary. This is usually made from one of the following materials:

(*a*) Tulasi wood. This plant, a member of the basil family, is considered a holy plant by the Hindus. It is grown in most Ashrams and also in private gardens and the scented leaves are offered in temples and eaten by the devotees as a form of prasada. Followers of the God Vishnu and his incarnations as Rama and Krishna use Malas made from tulasi wood.

(*b*) Sandalwood, according to tradition, is unsuitable for emotional people but used as Malas by others.

(*c*) Crystal beads are mostly used by devotees of the Divine Mother in her various forms (Shaktis). We are told that quartz or crystal beads, when used for any length of time, can become unbearable owing to their strong radiation.

(*d*) Rudraksha is a fruit growing in Nepal. Originally Malas made from this were worn exclusively by Sanyasins. Nowadays, however, they can be bought in shorter versions at Indian shops and are worn by many people.

The Malas, which are generally distributed by masters, are those made from Tulasi wood. Whenever a disciple is given Mantra-Diksha, he is given one of those Malas.

Mantras, which play such an important part in Yoga, are given by the priests at certain occasions. The first is given in childhood; the second when studying, or when achieving independence. The third when marrying and the fourth when wordly tasks have been completed and renunciation takes place. As not everybody becomes a renunciate, this, naturally, would be omitted. The last time man and Mantra meet is in the case of dying. Then a Mantra is recited by those attending the death.

Besides the more commonly known Mantras there are others for special occasions, or better for special purposes, such as snake bites, undesirable neighbours and other misfortunes. How serious their effect can be was experienced by Sir John Woodroffe, who acted as a judge in Calcutta. Dealing with a particular court case, he was appalled to notice that he was unable to give judgement. As this had never happened to him before, he began investigating and discovered that both parties concerned had been bombarding him with special Mantras to influence him in their favour. This was the beginning of his scientific career and he discovered that behind the Tantra-Shastra with the Mantra system lay a deep philosophical meaning which, up till then, had not been seriously considered by the West.

Tantra is originally a method of worship in relationship to the Divine Mother and it includes the use of Mantra and Yantra. Nowadays Tantra often has a bad overtone. In India one immediately thinks of black magic with its many tricks and methods for every situation in life. In the West one associates Tantra with the spilling of blood and sexual practices. But magic and orgies never were a path of Tantra: what happened is a mix-up of various elements. This kind of misunderstanding applies to the representation of copulating couples seen on carvings in Indian temples. These scenes have a spiritual meaning, which escapes the superficial tourist. They represent the god Shiva and his Shakti in the primeval state. These pairs are called Maithuna, a word which in Indian astrology stands for Gemini. In European esoteric tradition the highest state attainable is often represented by hermaphrodites or, in heraldry, it becomes a double-headed eagle. In Maithuna man and woman represent spirituality and materiality and their union is the final aim of all paths.

Many people assume that orgies and magic are a part of Tantra Yoga. That this is not the case will be understood when one considers the myth of the creation of the Tantra-Shastras:

One day Lord Shiva's wife, Parvati, felt full of compassion for all those people who were not living as hermits or in monasteries and therefore could not be saved. She begged her husband to find ways and means to show those unfortunates a path which would lead them to salvation. After long hesitation Shiva agreed and dictated the sixty-four Tantra-Shastras to her.

This myth tells us that meat-eaters, for example the warrior caste or Kshatriyas, were given a special technique to advance spiritually, in spite of their eating meat. Married people, by sublimating their sex life, were also included amongst those who can reach salvation.

This demonstrates that Yoga in all its aspects is part of man's ordinary life and was intended for people in various professions or trades. These people, in contrast to those who follow a spiritual path, are called Householders in India. Materiality must harmonize with spirituality; the Shakti, as Kundalini or Serpent Power, tarries at the root of the spine, waiting to join Shiva, resting in Sahasrara, the centre of the cerebrum, in a conscious stream of energy. Nowadays these two poles could be called genetic code and personal chains of associations.

When the world is created, the originally point-like pair separates and the life-force descends to the various dimensions of consciousness to give birth to the world. [Editor's note: Creation and dissolution of the world are cosmic processes which one experiences in the evolution of individual consciousness.] This manifesting power is called Kali. Subject and object divide and the world becomes Name (Nama), Sound (Shabda) and Form (Rupa). Although the same power forms the basis of everything, each individual thing has its own form and therefore all things are different.

In the process of meditation one retraces this path—the aim is the fusion of duality which is experienced as becoming one with the deity or as being absorbed into the cosmos. It is therefore wrong to indulge in romantic pantheism or the misunderstanding of Indian concepts.

In Tantra Yoga the goddess Kali or the life-force symbolizes the ascending and descending consciousness. This process follows a definite law by which all people and objects in the world are in a certain relationship to each other and to the whole cosmos. It is clear that one man differs from the next; having his own personal structure, he thinks and feels differently and stands in a different relationship to the cosmos than all other men. Yet there are main types with mutual characteristics which are stronger than the differences.

This cosmic law is symbolized by the necklace of Kali which consists of different syllables. Twelve syllables together, meaning the 'Name' or 'Sound' of the whole cosmos, are denoted by the root syllable OM. All the other syllables are aspects of this last principle and, as everybody is a different combination of the whole, a certain syllable or Mantra is particularly suitable for him; more than that—this syllable is a symbol for his personality. By repeating it, he repeats himself. This sound, repeated hundreds of times, becomes a permanent inner mirror reflecting oneself.

As the world not only manifests as sound but also as form, each Mantra should be accompanied by a Yantra or a form called Ishta Devata. In Indian tradition this is accepted as the figure of a favourite deity or the image of one's Guru. For the Western aspirant an abstract symbol, a flower, tree, animal, etc., as, of course, any sort of religious symbol, seems more appropriate. It is accepted that everybody has a particular form which he must discover himself and which *is* himself.

This form is needed when consciousness fades away into unconsciousness (that is, at the moment of Pratyahara).

The Mantra is usually given by a Guru, who, asking for the disciple's birth date, is able to recognize the individual combinations of a person. If there is no Guru available, a Mantra, corresponding with one of the five elements (see page 22) corresponding with the seeker's birth sign, can be chosen. [Editor's note: The Mantra which can be used by everyone is the sacred syllable OM.]

If, for some reason, a wrong Mantra has been chosen, it may have the same therapeutic effect as the correct Mantra, but it will be useless in deep meditation as, in this case, the subconscious is then programmed with only one part of the personality. This, though it would activate certain dispositions, will not help the integration of the various parts.

Technique

Take the Mala with the right hand between thumb and third or fourth finger. The second and fifth finger remain relaxed. Beginning with the bead next to the centre bead (marked with a little tuft), not too fast but not too slowly, shift one bead for each Mantra until you reach the beginning; the meru must not be crossed but with the same hand turn the Mala. The Mala is always held at the level of heart or knee, and each bead is moved in the direction of the palm towards the body. The left hand is used for counting, either allowing one finger for each Mala or one finger for three Malas, each joint of the finger representing one Mala. With each bead one either voices or thinks the Mantra. It must also correspond with the breathing; at the beginning this needs great concentration.

The Mantra itself should be co-ordinated with a particular Cakra, most often the Ajna Cakra. The following are the most important Bija-Mantras corresponding with the elements and their particular Cakras:

OM	= for Swamis or people who dedicate their life to the spiritual path	concentration on Ajna Cakra
Lam	= earth—for sentient people	Muladhara Cakra
Vam	= water—for emotional people	Svadhishthana Cakra
Ram	= fire—for people with will power	Manipura Cakra
Yam	= air—for thinkers	Anahata Cakra
Ham	= ether—for mature people with equipoise	Vishuddi Cakra

Besides these there are a great number of Mantras connected with various gods; the most important are the thirty-four Gayatri-Mantras. Here are two examples:

1. Om Ekadantaya Vidmahe Vakratundaya Dhimahi Tanno Danti Prachodayat.
2. Om Kalikayai Ca Vidmahe Shashanavasinyai Dhimahi Tanno Agora Prachodayat.

These Mantras are homages and prayers to the deities. Yogis usually use 'Om Nama Shivaya' which is meant to help the power of perseverance.

If you have chosen Manasika-Japa as your path and have gained experience in Japa-Yoga so that your subconscious can repeat the Mantra naturally and spontaneously, it is advisable to begin with Japa-Anushthana. Practically expressed this means that one takes a two weeks' holiday and practises for four hours in the morning, four hours in the afternoon and four hours at night. Then consider the following points:

1. Regular time, place, position and an equal number of Malas
2. Meticulous handling of Mala
3. Pleasant weather or a room with an even temperature
4. A light diet, not essentially vegetarian but a limited amount of food
5. A regular amount of time every day
6. Preferably advice from a Master who will stress details which vary according to the aim

Japa usually is a form of Sadhana or discipline, for the student of the spiritual path although it is often done to obtain material success or siddhis.

It is a hard and difficult undertaking, but the result is tremendous. After a few days one reaches a state which otherwise can only be experienced with the help of drugs, but in this case being 'high' has no side- or after-effects. The least which can be achieved by Manasika-Japa is to reach a state full of peace and harmony in which nothing can affect one any more.

Chapter 3

Trataka

Trataka is part of both the classical Hatha-Yoga as well as Raja-Yoga; this represents the physical part of Yoga which tries to reach the balance of 'HA', the left side of the body or the moon with 'THA', the right side of the body or the sun, as well as the royal or Raja-Yoga which uses Will as a vehicle.

Gheranda Rishi, the classic interpreter of Hatha-Yoga, considers Trataka as part of the 'Shatkarmas', the six cleansing exercises. It also strengthens the nerves and muscles of the eyes.

In Raja-Yoga Trataka serves as a preparation for Dharana. Trataka is the best exercise for retaining a symbol or form in meditation, when, in the state of Pratyahara, one would otherwise lose consciousness. 'Dharana' is usually translated as higher concentration—but this is misleading. Trataka, on the other hand, can be called concentration as the eyes are focused on an object. Dharana not only consists of inner concentration but it includes seeing and experiencing a form which, at that stage, cannot any more be disturbed by noise, inner restlessness, upsurging thoughts, etc. These distractions are already excluded at the level of Pratyahara. If the symbol, which is the form of awareness, is lost, awareness vanishes with it and one drowns in unconscious sleep.

In India, Trataka is employed as the most important exercise to achieve occult powers. In the Tantra methods it serves for the awakening of secret powers when it is combined with Mauna, the keeping of silence. When somebody keeps silence for a certain length of time everything he says afterwards will come true. This has less to do with power than with purity. If the subconscious becomes lightened in a person and he can see associations objectively, he simply realises what comes in the form of thought and expresses it; he therefore says only what is real—not that a thing becomes real because it has been said.

Trataka is practised in India on the following:

(1) Candle flame
(2) Black dot
(3) Symbol or Ishta-Devata
(4) Tip of the nose (Nasagra Drishti)
(5) Centre between the eyebrows (Bhrumadhya)
(6) Shiva-Linga*
(7) Sky or water
(8) Rising sun
(9) Sun
(10) Crystal
(11) Own shadow
(12) Darkness
(13) Emptiness (Shunya)
(14) Mirror
(15) One of the four elements
(16) One of the Cakras
(17) Inner form
(18) Yantra

* Shiva Linga, sign of Shiva, usually represented by an egg-shaped stone.

The first three are the most usual methods; (4) and (5) are only effective when perfect peace has been achieved and they then act directly on the Ajna or respectively the Sahasrara-Cakra; (11) and (14) are called Chaya-Upashana and are described in chapter 6. (17) is called Antar-Trataka (see chapter 4); all the others are more exercises of devotion rather than concentration, and (9), (12), (13), (15) and (16) ought to be taught by a 'Deshika', a Tantra Guru; (18) is taught in all the schools of Mahayana Buddhism, particularly in Tibet where the geometrical Yantras are replaced by painted Mandalas.

Trataka should always be followed by meditation on the Ishta-Devata in Cidakasha or Yoga-Nidra. People with spectacles should leave them off during these exercises.

Technique

Put the object of concentration at eye level and at a distance which enables you to see it very clearly. The body must be completely motionless, preferably in one of the positions of meditation. Breathing should be quiet, slow and normal. The eyes should be relaxed, not staring. When strain is felt, close them until they feel relaxed once more. You may see various colours and stars; watch them in a detached way, they are caused by the continuous pressure on the Ajna Cakra.

1. Watch the breath in the nose, how it rises and falls. Keep your eyes closed until you feel quiet and relaxed.
2. When doing Trataka on a candle flame, concentrate on the glowing point at the top of the wick. Avoid blinking—when your eyes begin to water or feel strained, close them immediately. While they are opened they should not feel tense. The aim is to keep them open *and* relaxed as long as possible (say, up to 15–20 minutes).
When doing Trataka on a black dot, this should be fixed on a wall.
3. Close your eyes: you may see many things but watch out for a star *without moving the eyes*. It will appear in the centre between the eyebrows and it will vanish and reappear several times. If it seems to go sideways or downwards, do *not* follow it with your eyes. When it has vanished entirely, open your eyes a second time and begin again with No. 2.
4. Once No. 3 has been mastered, a dark instead of a glowing star will appear; this moment is of special importance. It indicates movement in the dark, a dark centre. When this has been experienced, Trataka should be followed by Nada-Yoga (see chapter 8) instead of Yoga-Nidra or concentration on your symbol.

Indication

To begin with, one may not see anything owing to a lack of imagination; also one may find it difficult to visualize the star. If, after a certain time of practice, it still cannot be seen, look straight into a light bulb, then close the eyes and wait to see the reflection on the retina. If this does not help either, try another method of meditation. Perhaps your sense of hearing is more susceptible than your sense of vision and you should try Nada-Yoga. (See chapter 8.)

Chapter 4*

Antar-Trataka

'Antar' means inner. Antar-Trataka, a development of Trataka, is done without the help of objects. While Trataka produces physical results, particularly strengthening and cleansing of the vision, Antar-Trataka is an entirely mental exercise, widening and directing the inner sight. It can only be practised with real effect after long experience with Trataka. This meditation takes half an hour.

TEXT

Sit in the posture in which you feel most comfortable so that you can be immobile for half an hour.
Close your eyes
Relax   Sit straight   Spine upright
Hands on your knees
Now chant 'OM' seven times, loud, long and clear with fading 'MMM'
Bring your consciousness into the centre between the eyebrows, called Bhrumadya

The centre of the eyebrows
Go there with your consciousness.

Slowly, step by step   No tense effort—quietly

Concentrate awareness in the centre between the eyebrows

and if it seems difficult
lick your fourth finger and make a dot
with your fourth finger make a dot between your eyebrows.
Leave your finger there for a few seconds then remove it.

Remain very quiet.

Hold your consciousness at the centre between the eyebrows

Imagine a small star and see it, if possible
a small star between the eyebrows.

If you can see it good but if you can't, imagine it. Perhaps it will appear for a moment and then vanish, this does not matter. Concentrate on the star between the eyebrows. And when you can see the star watch it keep watching it. If you cannot see it but you can imagine it imagine a star in the sky surrounded by clouds a single small star in an endless sky it suddenly winks.

If you have no success, try it once more.

Wet your fourth finger with the tip of your tongue and touch Bhrumadya, the centre of the eyebrows. Leave the finger there for a few seconds and then entire awareness of Bhrumadya, the centre between the eyebrows. Imagine a small star or even better, see it. If you can see it, fix it but be relaxed. If you cannot see it imagine it. A tiny single star in the sky surrounded by black clouds

feel the star.

Imagine a dark dot or see it, in the same way as in Trataka, see the inner, pressing dot, the psychic germ which is a different colour in everybody, remember.

When you practise Trataka, what happens inside, when your eyes are closed? A small seed-like object, rising, sometimes glowing, sometimes pink, sometimes green with blurred outline.

Imagine this now and if possible see it.

If you can see it, continue, watch it but if you cannot, imagine a glowing seed, the psychic seed.

It becomes clearer and clearer in Bhrumadya, the centre of the eyebrows.

Awaken and retain this awareness of the psychic seed, the glowing point at the top of the wick and the bright seed.

Try your best to see the colour when you watch the glowing wick when you cannot see it, the bright seed, then imagine it, picture it.

Paint a small glowing seed, and, little by little bore a hole and it is possible and those, who know Trataka with the candle flame, ought to see or imagine

the flame of the candle

the golden flame of the candle

Try to see the flame if you can do it what does it look like at the top? A dot? Does it flicker in the eyes?

What does it look like at the bottom? Black? Green?

Try to discover it

And once more

if possible try to see yourself, your position, the candle, the burning candle, the breath passing through your nose, colours, all in front of you.

Draw this with your inner eye quickly.

The candle stands in front of you broader at the bottom narrower on top

a vertical white stick

standing in the dark
liquid wax dripping down its side, melting slowly.
The wick of the candle black and burning the white wick inside
the candle, turning black as it burns.
The wick is surrounded by the flame
surrounded by the flame
how is this?

The colour saffron?
brown? bronze?
golden?
Big? Small?
Look at it as sharply as possible.
Burning flame you feel the glowing point at
the tip of the slightly twisted wick.

It is not quite straight
but a little bent to the right.

It burns and this is the flame and it bends the wick a little to
the right or to the left
the flame has its shape
it is bent to the right
and you can see the flame, wider at the bottom and stretching
upwards higher upwards
you notice in the middle, where
the flame starts, a black smoky colour,
this is the source of light.

See yourself
in front of the candle
the melting of the wax
the dancing flame
the flame flickers a little
and you watch it.
Once more go into the centre between the eyebrows. Look at the star and imagine it. To see the star is the real

ANTAR-TRATAKA

After long practice, this inner star becomes a natural occurrence and its development is the development of your spiritual imagination. If you see the star in Bhrumadhya a psychic event it means that you have developed a new kind of vision.
Please understand this.
Without tension, as quickly as possible
concentrate all your attention on the centre between the eyebrows.
You can either press it or moisten it.
When you do this you will feel the pressure in a few seconds and the seed in you will become clearer and clearer.
The dot can be clearly felt, an inner pressure.
Those who can feel it, without outer help purely with their will power, do it without preparation.

star
small star
a small star
the burning point

which you have seen after Trataka, practice it, try to see
a burning point
look at it
in Bhrumadya, the centre between the eyebrows

then the flame
of the candle
look at the flame of the candle
on the column of the candle
and at the darkness behind

and the flame its colour around you you see the aura of the flame. Now make a great effort and bring it all into the centre between the eyebrows. Centre your consciousness there in a quiet flow. Remain awake there between the eyebrows. Collect all the sensations from all parts of your body and bring them into Bhrumadya. Fuse all your sensations in this point, life flowing there through many channels from all parts of your body. Incessant, concentrated awareness and sensation of Bhrumadya. This is ANTAR-TRATAKA in which you try to focus on the inner point which lastly is a star.

And something else in Bhrumadya you see
a human eye
a beautiful eye
an open........human eye
eyelids, eyelashes,
a perfect
human eye. You can see it, quite easily, it comes quickly,
the human eye.

And renewed, gather all life in yourself and allow it to flow into an eye.
And once more between the eyebrows there lives your own
third eye.
It is in your head, behind the skin, behind the bones, a living eye with a dull shine and it is an eyeball with blood. Deep inside? Oh yes!
You can see that it is deep inside you, behind the skin and the bones of the skull
In the depth of the space between the eyebrows a small eye which is closed.
Surrounded by muscles
as if enclosed by lips
as the mouth is closed so is the eye closed by muscles, it is quite closed. You can see that it is an eye from its shape and this is the third eye which can be developed the third eye which can be developed by this method is the tool to be used for inner imagination
Then you can see the Shiva-Linga those who know it can see it
The others imagine it:
In the middle of an oval base hollowed out in the centre stands an egg-shaped stone
it is quite simple an egg-shaped upright stone.
Imagine a temple or remember one you have seen and in it stands the Shiva-Linga, the stone
the symbol of the awakening, rising consciousness
Try to see it you can do it and then in the temple
the stone
a smooth flickering force.
Sit in front of the altar in this temple and there is
a shining crystal ball and you look into it.
This is you

the star
the flame
the dot
Shiva-Linga
the crystal ball, the third eye

IT IS YOU
HARI OM TAT SAT
HARI OM TAT SAT

Chapter 5*

Cidakasa-Vidya

Cidakasa-Vidya, also called Cidakasa-Dharana, is the experience of the inner space. To see one's inner space in all clarity means sharing an experience with sages and saints. They realize the wisdom of the cosmos contained in this space. Its colour is seen as dark blue or black. This practice belongs to one of the very oldest methods mentioned in the Vedas.

When using this technique, even a beginner can experience an inner reality. After some practice Cidakasa-Vidya forces an opening through which one penetrates into entirely new realms. The first aim is to see the inner darkness, visible when one closes the eyes, and to find a path along which one can lose the fear of this particular jungle. The final aim is to penetrate the darkness into the cosmic light. To reach this goal it is necessary to find a sense of orientation. The newly developed awareness will encounter various experiences arising from the subconscious or from reflexes of sense impressions. They can be seen in different colours and shades like stars, phosphorescent flashes, lightning or waves.

If one allows oneself to be distracted by these one will not be able to advance any further. Success depends on strict adherence to the text as otherwise it is easy to lose the way. Orderly penetration can only be achieved systematically.

The aim of this practice is to reverse the direction of vision. When seeing the world, one sees from inside to outside, but when looking inwards, the direction is from outside to inside. In the case of Cidakasa-Vidya the direction is from inside to even deeper inside, into the inner space, which means that the direction is pointing forward, but forward into the Cidakasa, that is an outer inside. The last step is reached when one has penetrated forward from the inner space to the centre. This cannot be explained any more but has to be experienced.

Cidakasa-Vidya is one of the most beautiful and one of the most relaxing techniques although it may be difficult for the beginner to remain motionless for a whole hour (this method cannot be practised lying down). If necessary, the time can be shortened to half an hour by omitting sections 1 to 4, but full results can only be achieved when the whole text has been used. It would be useless to try speeding up the reading; the speed must be finely balanced: each pause is important, and every word should be separated from the next and should emerge from the stillness.

TEXT

Prepare yourself   comfortable position   check everything
Legs crossed   hands on knees or comfortably linked
Spine erect   head straight   everything relaxed
To enable you to meditate easily   for some time without distraction without pain
Try to hear different sounds   outside   a clock ticking   a passing car   my voice   birds   twittering.
And suddenly feel your body   your whole body   complete awareness of your body   you must feel your physical being   the body   everything, the whole body.
And a constant stream of consciousness flowing   of physical being. Be sure that you feel the body
in its entity   not only single parts
but the whole shape of the body.
The more you feel it   the body   the quieter you become inside.

Nothing particular, not a single part of the body, but
consciousness of the whole, entirely.

Now switch over to the process of your breathing and at the same time remain conscious of your body. The uninterrupted flow of the sensation of physical being. In addition be conscious of your breathing, the normal natural breath, without any effort, as you look inside the breathing process, physical breath.

You are not doing it the breathing the breathing process is natural, and automatic. Sometimes deep, sometimes long, sometimes light, sometimes short and the breathing continues.

Awareness of breathing, the feeling of breathing with the feeling of the body.
And suddenly realize the essence, the substance itself
Cidakasa the space which is in you
space which penetrates every atom
of your body and spirit.
Space, which is neither inside nor outside but everywhere
It is not the space inside your forehead.
It is not the space above your head.
It is not the space behind your head.
It is not the space of your heart.
It is not the space of your belly or navel.
It is not the space of the lower body
but it is
the whole space
which contains
the physical being
as a whole.
If you feel Cidakasa you feel the space which is in the body, everywhere

in the body, penetrating the whole body, it includes the whole body, not any separate part of the body everything.

Feel Cidakasa the entity of your formless being the space which is around your body.

Its colour is black, it is without shape try to retain the colour of Cidakasa. What kind of colour is there in this Cidakasa?

Is it black? lighter than black? or another colour? It changes from moment to moment the colour in Cidakasa changes from colour to colour

If you watch carefully watch the colours which flow past you will think that they change very quickly. Sometimes it is difficult to keep pace with the floating colours and the vibrations of the colours.

Sometimes they are clear and sometimes they are blurred.

You cannot look through them, you cannot see them you cannot understand them.

These colours are not the same every day.

Tomorrow
the colours in this space
the colour inside will not be the same as now.

Try to stay aware of these quickly changing colours
colours
overpowering colours
supercharged clouds

passing through your Cidakasa
Cidakasa is being without shape
containing your physical being.

If you look at it, attentively, if you watch your Cidakasa, you will see waves of colour which flicker and quickly pass. These colours are symbols expressions of the stream of energy inside you.

These colours are symbols

expressions of the life-force

of the stream of energy in you.

Try to see the colours with their help and because of these colours a new knowledge will manifest in time. Cidakasa is life without form, the formless being, the formless reality

of your physical being.

1. It is not Cidakasa that you see in front of your forehead.
It is not Cidakasa that you see above the crown of your head.
It is not Cidakasa behind you.
It is not Cidakasa in the chamber of your heart

It is not your navel or back.

It is not Cidakasa in your lower body.
But that which contains the Cidakasa
everywhere
complete Cidakasa
Increase your sensations feel
Then watch the colours and tell yourself: I explore
observe
remember the colour?
When you can distinguish the colour, tell yourself: Red
blue
violet, etc.
If you cannot distinguish it, tell yourself: I cannot see anything.
Sometimes the colours are so blurred that it is impossible to decide what they are
But whether you can distinguish them or not, you ought to see the colours,

try
uninterruptedly this constant flow of your awareness
Direct it to the Cidakasa.
Do not allow do not allow yourself to be disturbed not the slightest interruption of your awareness.
Constant, uninterrupted, entire, spontaneous feeling of the whole Cidakasa.
which includes
all the yet unknown.
In this free space lives your body, Cidakasa is not the body
but the body is Cidakasa
Look into the Cidakasa and you will see lights, in different degrees, as zig-zags
a torrent
a vision
something
a thought
but inside, with all this, remain aware of the whole Cidakasa when you look ahead, ahead at your forehead, behind the bones, tell yourself: I wish to feel everything, the whole space.

2. First we must understand Cidakasa and when it is clear to us continue with the reading of the colours. When you have achieved this to read the colours,
bring yourself as a person into the centre of the eyebrows
and enter there through
a round opening.
Look at this cave
a round cave
and you see

IT IS A CAVE BUT YOU CANNOT ENTER IT!

Feel your physical being until you feel everything.
Awaken the sense of your body.
Visualize your body until you sense everything, you can be it

THE WHOLE

3. Now start normal breathing, constantly watch your breath, increasing awareness of the process of breathing, and simultaneously of the harmony of your body, both simultaneously
observation of breathing and sensing of the body.
This you must practise, the breath consciousness with true attention and care and quickly add the consciousness of the Cidakasa, the inner space, the outer space
the space which is infinite
incomprehensible
is the space in which you are.
Search for the colours, feel the colours.
Even if you are not capable of retaining the quickly changing colours it does not matter today but feel the colours come and go extremely fast from one moment to the next the colours change and you must watch with the greatest care and effort. They should be seen everywhere with every part of your body.

4. Realization of colour watching the colours pursuing the colours remembering the colours careful watching this is now your most important task in Cidakasa.

Remember again, when I say Cidakasa I do not mean the darkness or the inner firmament inside your forehead or above your head or behind your head
or behind
or in front
or below No!
I mean the whole thing, embracing everything all forms the awareness of the Cidakasa. When you can cope with this, it means that you can cope with a very special matter. When you understand Cidakasa, then you understand the substance of your physical existence and you can feel that you are able to sense your psyche.

(*End of half hour omission*)

Go to Bhrumadya between the eyebrows
Creep in and dig a round hole
dig a hole
with a round opening and look into it.
Step backwards and you see that it is dark inside.
Go nearer and enter
Oh it is very dark here. Nothing can be seen, nothing can be distinguished.
And when you have entered
when you have succeeded entering
then you cannot even see yourself
and this is deeper Cidakasa
Now repeat: OM
OM
OM
OM
OM
OM
OM

While you chant this OM, change the sound waves into fine psychic waves and feel your whole person in Cidakasa. Away from bodily awareness. Please understand this and do it. Whilst you repeat the OM, imagine, all around you, inside and everywhere else   the inner space   the darkness   the formless Cidakasa. And there appears a flickering light, a partial sensation of being. The body   please understand   the body seems to be the form of the sensation   this body appears in the form of the formless sensing.
Do it and repeat OM seven times

OM   OM   OM   OM   OM   OM   OM

Slowly come out

feel your body, the floor

then widen your awareness, listen
the movements and other things, the world around you and the words you hear.
Try to feel   be sure that you have come outside.
You realize the outer happenings
be sure that you hear and realize everything, sounds, the voice, the windows, the door, you yourself in a certain position in which you have just tried to experience Cidakasa.
Feel the head, the body,

arms, legs,
and everything else.
Open your eyes.
HARI OM TAT SAT

Chapter 6

Chaya-Upasana

Light is life and darkness is death.
Light—this is more than the sun, this is also the moon. Sun and moon, man and woman, animus and anima, Yang and Yin, Pingala and Ida of the Yogin—they all are the duality of spirituality and naturality which dwell in everything. Although they are positive and negative they are neither good nor bad. Light is white and darkness is black but both sun and moon produce light. Wherever there is something visible which seems clear, there is also another part covered with veils. Everything has its shadow, indivisibly connected, a grey mirror which lasts unto death. What is this, a shadow?

I am standing between it and its source, the origin, in which its end is already contained; if I were not standing here there would be light instead of the shadow, therefore I am both the cause and the creator of this faceless being.

The light from which I come I darken with my lack of knowledge, the creative source in myself is blocked and only in the dissolution of my person in death do I enter into the cosmic light which is the foundation of everything; so my person becomes creation and obstacle at the same time from and into the light with the body towards the sun. What I am within myself for the innermost light, that is my shadow.

It is a symbol for that which I am, what I see when I turn away from the light. In the cave image of Plato the shadows represent the world, and that which throws the shadows represents ideas. Even in death it will remain with me, dividing itself into elements, as my body disintegrates. I almost want to say that I am the shadow—should I now turn towards it, the darkness, or should I turn towards the light?

I then look into the mirror, there is the brightness which, or what I am; the shadow is the unilluminated mirror and the mirror is both a bright darkness and light hiding my form. There I see the shadow and I see it with features, outlines, colour, the tendencies in the symbol of my body and my face.

The quest for the shadow becomes a quest for the light. Those for whom light only represents light, without mystery, for them the shadow may represent a matter of course. The path of meditation is the path through darkness to the light, faced by the shadow of the subconscious.

Is this shadow the subconscious as an expression of my body, or of my spirit or perhaps of my soul?

In India, there exist astrologers who measure the shadow before casting a horoscope. People using a pendulum say that the human shadow possesses an aura which has a certain variable radiation. The shadows of the dead do not have an aura; life can be measured on the shadow in the same way as on the living body. When the soul of man 'escapes' with death, the shadow ought to vanish as well, yet dead bodies throw shadows in the same way as living bodies. What is it now, this shadow?

Could it be a part which has not yet become light, the part of man which has not yet been purified fading away into the dark? But saints, too, have shadows; so has every living creature and even inanimate objects throw shadows. During dreams the world does not cast shadows; the world of dreams has been caught in fairy tales and there the shadow is always something special. Innumerable stories tell of people who have sold or pawned their shadow to the devil, to death, or to a ghostly being, to get something in exchange for it. In the story 'The Fisherman and his Soul' Oscar Wilde says, 'What people call the shadow of the body is not the physical body's shadow but it is the body of the soul.' This story tells how a young fisherman wants to get rid of his soul to be united with a mermaid whom he loves. When, according to the instructions of a witch, he cut away his shadow from around his feet, it rose up and stood before him and looked at him. The soul or the shadow constantly tries to re-enter the fisherman and at the end of the story he is united in death with his beloved and his soul.

In the same story his soul wanders and reaches the realm of wisdom. There, after some difficulties, it is taken into the sanctuary where the Divine Being lives. 'Again the priest trembled and led me into the third chamber, and lo! there was no idol in it, nor images of any kind, but only a mirror of round metal set on an altar of stone. And I said to the priest: "Where is the god?" and he answered me: "There is no god but this mirror that thou seest, for this is the Mirror of Wisdom. And it reflecteth all things that are in heaven and on earth, save only the face of him who looketh into it. This it reflecteth not so that he who looketh into it may be wise. Many other mirrors are there, but they are the mirrors of Opinion. This only is the Mirror of Wisdom. Therefore we accept it as the god and we worship it." And I looked into the mirror and it was even as he said to me: I then did a strange thing but it matters not what I did.'

Although Oscar Wilde called the shadow the soul, he meant something different. It is important in this connection that the detached shadow of the fisherman was 'as himself', meaning a reflection in the mirror, yet in the mirror of wisdom everything else but the face is reflected.

My reflection in the mirror is my own shadow in the light; in darkness the mirror becomes the mirror of the shadow. Both mirror and shadow are polar but do not represent duality such as sun and moon, or other traditional aspects of creation or being.

My mirror image is the image of myself with my own identifications, the 'opinions', that which seems to be; my shadow is my image in the state of featurelessness, but not yet clarified. Maybe one ought to join these two, as shadow and mirror image together are oneself, seen from two final points which have to be integrated.

Chaya-Upashana means literally 'to sit next to the shadow'. In Chaya-Upashana one's own shadow or one's reflection in the mirror becomes the object of contemplation. There are several variations: in the first one endeavours to sense one's shadow with closed eyes and from this inner image one's own face emerges and the aura becomes visible. In the second the reflection of one's face in the mirror becomes the field of meditation; this vanishes and gets blurred and shadows or other faces take its place.

In the meditation on the shadow the 'real' image comes to the surface and in the mirror meditation the shadow appears in the real image. This means that a process of integration or clarification is taking place. The shadow represents the figure of a person without attributes, that is in the shadow one sees oneself as a manifesting density without the veiling masks of inclinations and everything else which one considers personality. This is indicated in the well-known and oft-interpreted fairy tale about a shadow, 'Peter Schlemihl' by Adalbert Chamisso. Schlemihl exchanges his shadow for inexhaustible wealth, becoming richer than anybody else, but he loses adaptability to his surroundings. The loss of the shadow symbolizes the loss of self-evidence. People do not resent another person's riches but they do resent somebody who is different. The devil is almost sure of Schlemihl and offers him, as the last exchange, to return his shadow for his soul. When Schlemihl refuses this transaction and at the same time renounces his wealth, he gains his freedom by obtaining the seven-league boots. With these he explores the whole world.

In meditation one does not only experience the How (the features) but also the What (the density). One can also experience it in mirror meditation although this may be accompanied by undesirable phases during which the subconscious rises to the surface. In this confrontation the path of meditation turns into psychological self-analysis.

C. G. Jung writes that during the dialectic process in alchemy (which is nothing else than projected meditation), the adept consequently has to face his own shadow. He calls it the dark half of his soul which somehow or other one has to get rid of, be it through penitence or through transference to one's neighbour.

In alchemy this first step will be felt as 'melancholy'; the evil of the world will be experienced as part of one's own personality. The union with this shadow is the aim of alchemy.

The shadow, as in the story of Schlemihl is a negative I-personality which encloses regrettable and uncomfortable attributes. Integration can only be achieved by the unyielding acceptance of the mirror-I.

Mirror meditation should only be practised after a certain preparation and then, under guidance, it should be practised continuously.

At the beginning Chaya-Upasana has the same advantages as Trataka as it is a preparation to cross the threshold between Pratyahara and Dharana. It ought not to be practised for more than twenty minutes.

Technique

1. (*a*) In a sitting position and entirely relaxed, concentrate on the Vishuddhi-Cakra in your shadow, thrown either on the floor or on a wall. (The shadow can be produced either by sunlight or a lamp.)
   (*b*) Close the eyes when they begin to hurt or to water. With the inner eye follow the outline of the shadow (in fact its reflex imagine on the retina. There is a tendency to follow the outline of the shadow by moving the eyes although they are closed. This should be avoided.) When the picture becomes blurred or vanishes, repeat from the beginning.
   (*c*) Sometimes the darkness of the shadow becomes lighter and changes to pale silvery grey, surrounded by rays in all colours. Watch these happenings in a completely detached way.
   (*d*) When the picture can be seen calmly and clearly, the colours will gradually vanish to make way for a single colour which is the colour of one's own aura.
2. The same process can be repeated but instead of concentrating on the shadow, use a mirror. In this case fix your eyes on Bhrumadhya not on Vishuddhi-Cakra.

Gradually, in fully concentrated relaxation, the aura becomes visible to the open eyes. When perfection of the technique has been reached, it is possible to see other peoples' auras.

3. This can be done either in a sitting or standing position. The process is the same as in 1 (*a*) and 1 (*b*) but the head is thrown back and the reflection will be seen on a cloudless sky or, if this is not possible, on the ceiling.

In classic traditional Yoga this reflection will be defined as a body of smoke which partly corresponds with our conception of the subconscious.

Chapter 7*

Yoga-Nidra

'Nidra' means sleep and Yoga-Nidra is the sleep of the Yogi. This easy and effective method has often been explained as a kind of hypnosis, and some of the stages do resemble hypnosis in a certain way, particularly at the beginning as one sinks into darkness from which the words seem to emerge. Although Yoga-Nidra offers an easy way into sleep, the art of it is to remain fully conscious throughout and to resist the temptation to fall asleep.

Yoga-Nidra is practised lying down, preferably on the floor on a rug or carpet or, if it is not too soft, on a bed. One must lie completely flat without a pillow but it is advisable to cover oneself with a blanket, since one otherwise feels cold as the body relaxes. The room should have a pleasant temperature and Yoga Nidra should not be practised in the open air where one might be disturbed by insects or even a slight breeze. The most important aspect is the entire immobility of the body. Half an hour of Yoga-Nidra replaces up to several hours of sleep, according to the depth one reaches. A person practising Yoga-Nidra will appear to be in a deep sleep; sometimes although conscious he may even snore.

The voice of the teacher or one's own voice on a tape is the rope on which one descends into a deep chasm. If one is inattentive for even a single moment, one falls into deep darkness, one plunges into unconsciousness or falls asleep. Whereas in other methods one tries to penetrate the threshold of the unconscious, in Yoga-Nidra the gate leading into the unconscious is thrust open.

In perfect Yoga-Nidra (second variation) the whole personality has reached the source. At the beginning of it, and again at the end, one makes a resolution, the Sankalpa. This must not concern anything trivial but be a direction for one's whole life. It is best to listen within and to wait for it. It must not be changed until it has become realized. This resolve is incredibly powerful and always, without doubt, comes true, as it programmes the subconscious and directs all actions to this aim.

The first variation takes about half an hour. The complete second variation takes approximately three times as long, but it can be reduced to one hour. In both variations the eyes must be kept closed throughout; after completion one should sit up slowly, turn to the right, and only then open the eyes.

Outer reality is excluded in deep Yoga-Nidra, yet consciousness remains clear. This awareness is similar to the state of sleeplessness, yet without the other results such as becoming overtired, nervous and strained. On the contrary—one feels relaxed and refreshed after practice.

When working without guidance one should not try to remember the single stages (especially in variation 2). Everything ought to sink into the subconscious, so that later on the process happens mechanically, particularly if needed to combat insomnia.

Practise the first variation at the beginning until you can remain relaxed throughout, finding the right balance between sleep and disciplined attention. It will take about a month to reach proficiency.

Later on begin with the second variation.

TEXT

First Variation

HARI OM HARI OM

Lie down, be comfortable

Relax relax no more movement

Close your eyes   no more movement
Entire tranquility for Yoga-Nidra   the sleepless sleep
Allow yourself to sink more and more into the ground
                                   but remain awake
The relaxation embraces everything, the ground, the air, the body
The whole body,   mind,   emotions
Everything fuses into harmony.
Everything is relaxed, as before going to sleep
But remain conscious!   aware!   attentive!   ready!
Feel your whole body.
Divide the consciousness simultaneously   evenly   in the whole body lying on the floor
And now concentrate on those parts of the body which touch the floor. Feel the areas of contact with the floor:

the right heel   where it touches the floor
the left heel   where it touches the floor
right calf   where it touches the floor
left calf   where it touches the floor
right thigh   where it touches the floor
left thigh   where it touches the floor
right buttock   where it touches the floor
left buttock   where it touches the floor
small of the back   where it touches the floor
back   where it touches the floor
right shoulder blade   where it touches the floor
left shoulder blade   where it touches the floor
right hand   where it touches the floor

left hand where it touches the floor
right elbow where it touches the floor
left elbow where it touches the floor
back of the neck where it touches the floor
back of the head where it touches the floor

The whole area of contact of the body with the floor
Sensation of all points of contact simultaneously evenly.
intensive, exclusive sensation of the area of contact of the body with the floor
the floor body—floor
Incessantly body—floor
Incessant sensing body—floor
Penetrating awareness body—floor
Continue body—floor
Meeting points body—floor
Concentrate your whole strength on the area of contact
The meeting points, the floor on which you rest
Concentration on this area of strength
Concentration on this area of strength
Still more
Still more intensively
Awareness of the floor, the meeting points of the area of strength
And now bring your attention to the eyelids
Feel the line, the narrow line, where upper and lower eyelids meet feel where they touch feel the 'between' of the meeting, concentration on line of meeting, concentration on the between And now the line of contact of the lips the meeting of the lips centre your whole attention on this place where upper and lower lips meet complete concentration actual touch the meeting, feel the nothing between both lips

Then once again feel the contact area between body and floor
Feel the centre of gravity in this area of contact the point of the most intensive contact feel it!
Now feel the flow of your breath, the quiet breath and imagine you breathe in through the left nostril and out through the right nostril. In through the right and out through the left. Now count attentively:

1. Inhale left — 1. Exhale right
2. Inhale right — 2. Exhale left
3. Inhale left — 3. Exhale right
4. Inhale right — 4. Exhale left
5. Inhale through both
5. Exhale through both
6. Inhale left — 6. Exhale right
7. Inhale right — 7. Exhale left
8. Inhale left — 8. Exhale right
9. Inhale right — 9. Exhale left
10. Inhale through both
10. Exhale through both

Continue:

11. Inhale left — 11. Exhale right
12. Inhale right — 12. Exhale left
13. Inhale left — 13. Exhale right
14. Inhale right — 14. Exhale left
15. Inhale through both
15. Exhale through both

And again:

16.	Inhale left	16.	Exhale right
17.	Inhale right	17.	Exhale left
18.	Inhale left	18.	Exhale right
19.	Inhale right	19.	Exhale left

20. Inhale through both
20. Exhale through both

21—21 (mentally counting in the rythm of breathing)
22—22, 23—23, 24—24, both 25—25, 26—26, 27—27,
28—28, 29—29, both 30—30, 31—31, 32—32,
33—33, 34—34, both 35—35, 36—36, 37—37,

(*2 minutes pause*)

Look into the darkness of the inner space, feel the space inside your head, look from inside at the wall behind your forehead, feel the wide space

Out of the darkness a mirror arises a square mirror in front of you framed the mirror

and there you see yourself, your face

To the smallest detail
Your quiet face in the inner mirror
Look at mirror and face
Look at every detail

HARI OM TAT SAT

Slowly open your eyes, turn to the right and sit up (end)

Second Variation

Lie down   be comfortable
Close your eyes   relax   complete immobility
No more movement   complete immobility
Relax the body but remain attentive throughout
Practise alternate breathing:
Breathe in through the left nostril and breathe out through the right.
In right,   out left,
Every fifth time inhale and exhale through both nostrils
Conscious and clear mental counting   Listen inside to the sound of each number, watch each number   wait

1. left in   1. right out
2. right in   2. left out
3. left in   3. right out
4. right in   4. left out

5. both in
5. both out
Continue by yourself

(*2 minutes pause*)

And now Sankalpa (resolution)
Make a resolution   a resolution   formulate it quite clearly and simply formulate it mentally clear and exact

Repeat your resolution three times

The resolution which you repeat three times before and three times after Yoga-Nidra will, without any doubt, come true.

Now begin Yoga-Nidra

by rotating the consciousness through the body
as quickly as possible

Do not only think of the various parts of the body, but feel them.

1. We go with our thoughts and with our whole attention to each part of the body mentioned now:

Right Hand:

thumb: tip, nail, first joint, knuckle
1st finger: tip, nail, first joint, second joint, third joint
2nd finger: tip, nail, first joint, second joint, third joint
3rd finger: tip, nail, first joint, second joint, third joint
4th finger: tip, nail, first joint, second joint, third joint
palm, little mounds of the palm: one, two, three, four, five
back of the hand: knuckles, wrist, forearm, elbow, upper arm, shoulder, armpit

Left Hand:

As right hand.

Right Foot:

big toe, second toe, third toe, fourth toe, fifth toe, sole, heel, instep, ankle, calf, shin, knee, thigh, hip

Left Foot:

As right foot.
Then:

Back:

right buttock	. . .	left buttock
small of the back	. . .	the whole back
right ribcage	. . .	left ribcage
right shoulder blade	. . .	left shoulder blade
back of the neck	. . .	back of the head
crown of the head	. . .	forehead
right eyebrow	. . .	left eyebrow
centre between the eyebrows	. . .	Bhrumadya, the centre between the eyebrows
right eye	. . .	left eye
right cheek	. . .	left cheek
right ear	. . .	left ear
nose	. . .	tip of the nose
right nostril	. . .	left nostril
upper lip	. . .	lower lip
chin	. . .	throat
right collarbone	. . .	left collarbone
right breast	. . .	left breast
abdomen	. . .	navel
right groin	. . .	left groin
the whole right leg	. . .	the whole left leg
the whole right arm	. . .	the whole left arm
the whole body	the whole body	the whole body
the whole body	the whole body	the whole body

(Repeat from 1. Once or twice.)

2. Beginning at the tips of the toes allow consciousness to rise slowly along the body as if you were removing a veil;
Toes—feet—calves—both knees—thighs—hips—waist—abdomen—chest—both arms —shoulders—head.
Now consciousness radiates through the whole body.
Awaken the sensation of heaviness in various parts of the body, feel the heaviness in every single part of the body.

(Repeat from 1 to 2. Up to 5 times.)

Now awaken the sensation of weightlessness in all parts of the body. Feel how light you are, every part of the body floating.

(Repeat 1.–2. once or twice.)

(*half a minute pause*)

Awaken the sensation of heat. Try to experience heat.
Summer, sun and heat on the beach
Some kind of experience of very strong heat.

heat in the right leg	heat in the left leg
heat in the right arm	heat in the left arm
heat in the right sole	heat in the left sole
heat in the right palm	heat in the left palm
heat in the right eye	heat in the left eye

The whole body is hot
the whole body is hot
the whole body is hot
the whole body is hot
the whole body is hot
the whole body is hot
the whole body is hot

(*half a minute pause*)

Awaken the sensation of cold, bitter cold, remember the bitter cold in the winter—you walk barefoot in the snow—on a very cold floor, on ice.

Awaken the sensation of cold in the feet
cold in the spine
cold in the hands
cold in the arms
cold in the knees, cold in the thighs, cold in the buttocks, cold in the head, cold in the whole body—cold in the whole body—cold in the whole body—cold in the whole body—cold in the whole body—cold in the whole body—cold in the whole body

(*quarter-minute pause*)

Imagine pain, a certain pain which is familiar to you,
experience it in the teeth, in the stomach, in the spine or wherever you can imagine it best.

(*quarter-minute pause*)

Experience joy, great pleasure, remember a particular kind of enjoyment and try to re-experience it entirely, whether it is your favourite dish, enjoyment of swimming, love, flying or lying on the beach.

(*quarter-minute pause*)

Now localize the centres of energy:

Muladhara — at the root of the spine, between anus and urethra
Svadhishthana — second vertebra above coccyx
Manipura — at the level of the navel in the spine

Anahata	—	at the level of the heart in the spine
Vishuddhi	—	at the nape of the neck
Ajna	—	at the level of the centre between the eyebrows inside the head
Bindu	—	at the back of the head, 3 centimetres from the place where monks have the tonsure and Brahmins wear a tuft of hair
Sahasrara	—	at the crown of the head, penetrating into the centre of the brain

And now backwards:

Sahasrara—centre of the brain, Bindu—back of head, Ajna—inside the head, Vishuddhi—nape of neck, Anahata—level of heart, Manipura—level of navel, Svadhishthana—above coccyx, Muladhara—root cakra.
Muladhara—Svadhishthana—Manipura—Anahata—Vishuddhi—Ajna—Bindu—Sahasrara—Bindu—Ajna—Vishuddhi—Anahata—Manipura—Svadhishthana—Muladhara—Svadhishthana—Manipura—Anahata—Vishuddhi—Ajna—Bindu—Sahasrara—Bindu—Ajna—Vishuddhi—Anahata—Manipura—Svadhishthana—Muladhara.

Now concentrate on the Cakras and visualize them as their symbols:

Muladhara	—	a red triangle, apex downwards, inside the triangle there is a snake coiled three and a half times, its head pointing upwards
Svadhishthana	—	dark night, sleep
Manipura	—	glowing yellow, sunflower (lotus)
Anahata	—	a small flickering lamp
Vishuddhi	—	sensation of cold—a drop of nectar
Ajna	—	a state of being dazed and half asleep
Bindu	—	waxing moon in a starlit night
Sahasrara	—	a thousand-petalled lotus with the Shiva-Linga prominent in the centre (an egg-shaped, upright stone)

Muladhara—red triangle, snake; Svadhishthana—unconsciousness; Manipura—sunflower, lotus; Anahata—small lamp; Vishuddhi—drop of nectar; Ajna—being dazed; Bindu—moon; Sahasrara—Shiva-Linga; Bindu—moon; Ajna—being dazed; Vishuddhi—drop of nectar; Anahata—small lamp; Manipura—sunflower; Svadhishthana—darkness; Muladhara—triangle, snake.

(Repeat twice from Muladhara to Sahasrara and back.)

Now visualize the following:
A castle—a bell tower—a moving car—a galloping horse—a landscape in the sun at midday—a street lantern—a coconut tree—black clouds—a brown dog—sun rise—sun set—a red rose—a violet orchid—the bank of a river—a human skeleton—a birch tree in a garden—the meditating Buddha—a tennis racket—a pewter dish—a begging monk—a mill on a river—Father Christmas—a mountain brook—your own outstretched physical body, naked, lying in front of you, connected by a silver cord with your transparent, mental body; look at your outstretched body

You are now inside the transparent body and you look at your outstretched physical body. From the navel of the transparent body a golden cord rises into the sky and there floats your third body—cloudy, smoky—and embedded in this body
in this third body
lies the fourth
golden body
radiant like the sun

Think of your brain, deep, deep in the brain; in the centre there lies a golden egg, deep inside. Penetrate into the golden egg. Seven threads of a spider's web in a glittering misty wood—a golden bird above a lake—a coniferous forest—an aeroplane—a power plant—an ant—a crystal goblet—an old library—west wind—something crawls slowly up your spine—you are sitting in Padmasana—you are standing on your head—you are sitting in a glade in front of a Swami, looking into his eyes—he is directing you—you are feeling Prana, the life-force flowing into your body and you see your own radiation, the aura. Is it brown? green? red? yellow or orange? In front of you is a big garden in which men and beasts are living peacefully together

and you hear OM OM OM

A sacrificial fire—smoke rising from the chimney of a hut—the scent of lilac—
Ask yourself; Am I awake? Am I asleep?
And again

Feel your brain
Deep inside your brain
The golden egg—radiant

Look sharply at the golden egg inside you

This is yourself

(*quarter-minute pause*)

Hear the sound of the sea—thunder—a snowscape—radiant sun

HARI OM TAT SAT HARI OM TAT SAT HARI OM TAT SAT

Contract your muscles, breathe in deeply
Sit up slowly, eyes remain closed
Repeat your resolution three times
Repeat your resolution three times
your Sankalpa
Yoga-Nidra is finished—open your eyes.

Chapter 8

Nada-Yoga

People to whom sound means more than any other sense perception, for example, blind people, musicians or musicologists, will find the ideal path in Nada-Yoga.

The word Nada is derived from the Sanskrit root NAD, which means flowing. The same word also means sound. Nada-Yoga represents a flowing action, in this particular case the flow of consciousness.

The technique of Nada-Yoga consists of consciousness following a succession of sounds. There are four stages in this process corresponding with the four steps of tonal manifestations; they are called Vaikhari, Madhyama, Pashyanti and Para.

Vaikhari	is a tone either produced by striking two objects, or by striking a chord. Our language and music come under this concept.
Madhyama	(This means 'between', a tone between an audible and inaudible sound.) It is a subtle tone, a whisper, which produces almost no audible effect.
Pasyanti	is a kind of mental tone; one could say a tone which cannot be heard, but can be seen. Pasyanti means 'visible' or 'imaginable'. How can one see a tone? Have you ever heard music in a dream? Or has a melody haunted you sometimes? Pasyanti indicates this particular dimension. It is a sound which is nearer to your mind than to your ear.

Para — is the inaudible sound or the audible silence. It is more than ordinary silence which happens when nothing is heard—it is an *inner* silence, which can be experienced as the root sound or the possibility of a sound. Para is the last stage in deepest meditation before it becomes Samadhi. A sound without vibration or with an infinite wave length. Para means 'transcendental' or 'beyond'.

Para also describes a tone outside the Andolanas, the concept of vibration rate in Indian music. Para does not represent those sounds which lie either above or below the threshold of audible sound, those sounds which, although they can be produced, are not discernible for the human ear. In the scriptures referring to Para it is said that this has neither frequency nor movement nor vibration.

For the Pythagoreans this sound stood for the nought or it represented the junction of the Chi. Harmonically speaking, the path to the cosmic sound leads to the rays of creation, the diagonals, to the cosmic source.

In the holy texts of the Indians, the Upanishads, the sound of OM is called the purest manifestation of Para. This does not indicate the chanted OM but the OM in its most subtle form which changes into formlessness. The Upanishads distinguish this with the words: 'That is OM and this sound is OM'.

The nature of the OM becomes Jyotihr, meaning the innermost light. This is a centre in which the world of colour and sound is ruled by the same law. In meditation light and silence are identical.

Para cannot be grasped through a sense organ but it is a quality of purest consciousness.

From the living experience of Nada-Yogis a world system was created, similar to the system of the Pythagoreans. In the Indian pantheon of the gods the last transcendental sound of Para is accepted on the same level as the cosmic source and it is called Para—Brahman. It is the seed from which the worlds were created and developed. The 'Word' of the Bible: In the beginning was the Word and the Word was with God and the Word was God (John 1: 1), is called Nada or Shabda; Indian Sufis call it Surat.

Surat-Shabdha-Yoga is another name for Nada-Yoga. Nada-Yogis believe that the five elements (earth, water, fire, air and ether), five Karmendriyas (organs of action), and the five Jnanendriyas (sense organs or those concerned with thought), the four-fold mind and the three Gunas (original qualities), have all developed from one infinite sound. In other words the creation of the world has unfolded itself according to the cosmic law of sound (otherwise called Prakriti). This means that reality becomes manifested vibration.

Whoever wants to go deeper into these up-to-date theories should study the Nada-Bindu-Upanishad and the Hamsa-Upanishad both of which deal with them.

There are several other communities and sects, specializing in Nada-Yoga. The best known are the Radha-Swamis and snake charmers. Indian music, too, in its classic expression, follows the law of the Nada system. The well-known Sama-Veda is chanted with scientific precision and corresponds with Nada-Yoga. Indian music is co-ordinated to the fact that certain Nada frequencies correspond with particular moods. Nada vibrations and particular successions of tones or Ragas ought to be played at certain times, whereas for other hours different Ragas should be used.

To give an example: Diurnal people usually like Bhairavi-Ragas, while nocturnal people prefer Malkos-, Jogia-Ragas, Kaunsi Kanada-Ragas, as well as Durga-Ragas. Young people mostly prefer Bhairavi-Ragas. The effect can only be felt if the music is listened to for several hours. In preparation for meditation music could play a very important part.

One of the famous Indian saints, Kabir, whose songs became known in the West through the translations of Rabindranath Tagore, was a Nada Yogi; in one of his songs he says:

> Who plays the flute in the centre of the sky?
> At the point where the Ganges and Jamuna meet
> somebody plays the flute.

And the confluence of the three rivers, Ganges,
Jamuna and Sarasvati, is in Trikuti.
Oh! This is the junction of Ganges and Jamuna
The sound emerges from the North
Milkmaids hear it and are spellbound by these sounds.

This theme is elaborated in one of the great books of India, the Bhagavata-Purana:

God Krishna left his abode
And ran into the jungle.
It was the night of the full moon in the first month of winter
He took his flute and began to play.
The echo of sounds flowed into the silence of the night
And rose from the wild thicket
Awakening the Gopis (milkmaids)
And as they heard the sounds they left their houses
And their husbands and hurried, forgetting everything else,
Without care they ran from where rose the Nada of the flute,
They then began to dance wildly around the God
Soon each of them had danced with Krishna.

An imaginative fairy tale—but more than that, as it describes a certain condition of consciousness in allegorical form. The flute playing of Krishna is the Nada-Sadhana, the layer of consciousness where, from deep inside, a sound calls, until the senses (Gopis) forget the outer reality (their husbands) and withdraw from their sense organs to dance around the point-like sound. In Yoga this moment is described as 'Dharana has started and Dhyana is dawning'.

Etymologically speaking, Krishna is 'that which draws' or 'that which attracts'. The root of the word is Karsh. Krishna is therefore a person who acts like a magnet; the word Gopi comes from 'go' which means senses or cow, but also modest, poor.

In everyday language a Gopi is the daughter of a family of cow herdsmen, but esoterically it means the senses. Their husbands represent the world of outer reality.

A forest stands for the inner reality and the moonlit night indicates the Bindu-Cakra which, in Nada-Yoga is the centre of awareness. In Yoga the state described above is called advanced Pratyahara.

In Indian mythology the same layer of consciousness is also symbolized in the sage Narada who is closely linked with Krishna. This Rishi is represented with a vina (a lute) in his hand. In a similar state of consciousness the tone of this vina can be heard like the tone of a flute. When tones of murli (flute) or vina are mentioned, it is clear that these tones belong to the Pasyanti state. Here we must stress that these tones are not hallucinations but reality. We are dealing with symbols for the contents of mind and consciousness. They can be understood as vibrations of different realms of one's own being.

It is important to mention in this connection that the brain waves picked up by encephalographs can be as low as sine waves between 1 and 30 c.p.s. This is the field of sound waves; those under 16 c.p.s., although not audible to the human ear, still conform with the natural laws of musical sounds. In Nada-Yoga-Sadhana one learns to experience the realms of these vibrations first over the 'somatic sensations of harmony'. To be exact, then one does not hear the sounds any more but one senses frequencies which can be described as sounds of flutes or bells.

In this process one crosses various levels and these different 'bodies' are divided into a system in Yoga; one speaks of different Kosas, the Annamaya-, Pranamaya-, Manomaya-, Vijnanamaya- and Anandamaya-Kosas. The first realm belongs to the body consisting of nourishment and the energy of Prana (the Sthulasarira or dense body); the next three realms are made from mental and astral materials (the Sukshma-Sarira or the finer body) and the last realm consists of pure happiness and joy (the

Karana-Sarira or cosmic body). This three-fold body therefore consists of five levels of energy and in each of these realms one hears different sounds. In the first realm it is still comparatively easy to say from where they come: the heartbeat, breath in the lungs, sounds of circulation of the blood and those inside the head. The last experience in Nada-Yoga is higher than those created by flute or lute.

The primeval sound in this last realm is called Anahada-Nada. Here a misunderstanding ought to be clarified. Anahada is sometimes mistaken for Anahata-Nada. 'An' means not and 'ahat' means tapping or beating. Anahata therefore means 'not beating' and it describes the step from Vaikhari to Madhyama sounds. One of the most famous Koans in Zen meditation indicates this quite clearly; the aspirant is told to listen to the clapping of both his hands and afterwards to hear the clapping of a single hand. This is not just a paradox but can be experienced. Anahada means 'without boundaries' or 'without quality', indicating that we are dealing with a non-tone.

In meditation the Nada-Yogis follow the sounds to a point-like centre at their innermost depth. This centre appears also in other techniques. Bhaktas, Yogis of devotion, search for this centre of their Ishta (Divine form) in the Anahata Cakra. Jnana Yogis search for the centre of highest intuition in the Ajna Cakra (Third eye). Vedantins search for the centre of Hiranya-Garbha in the Sahasrara Cakra. Nada-Yogis search for the centre of Para-Nada in the Bindu Cakra.

Technique

1. Preparation

   (*a*) Sit in Padmasana or Vajrasana and practise Yoga Mudra for two minutes.
   (*b*) Practise Mulabandha fifty times.
   (*c*) Pranayama: Five rounds of alternate breathing for the purification of the Nadis (psychic nerve channels), then seven Brahmari (the bee) as follows:

After deep inhalation close ears and eyes covering them both with thumbs and forefingers and produce a humming sound with the exhalation, simultaneously concentrating on the Bindu Cakra.

2. Sit in one of the meditation postures. Close ears with your thumbs, supporting elbows on your knees or on a small table (cotton-wool or earplugs could be used instead of fingers). With closed eyes concentrate on the Bindu-Cakra and try to hear something.
3. The emerging sound can vary: you might hear a bell, twittering birds, thunder, the pounding of the sea, the twanging of a guitar or something else. At the beginning it is difficult to hear anything as one does not yet realize how it should be heard.

If you have difficulties in hearing while concentrating on Bindu, search around inside your head or concentrate on the heartbeat. Finally you should be able to hear the sound in Bindu, although it is tempting to listen to it at other points but do not give in to this as your progress in meditation depends on this particular experience.

4. When you are able to hear a sound in Bindu, try to hear it clearer and more distinctly. Soon there will be a second, different, sound in the background, parallel with the first. Cease listening to the first sound and try to follow the second one until this, too, becomes clear and the first sound vanishes altogether. Now listen to the next sound and treat it in the same way as the previous one and continue like this. If after the third sound the first sound emerges again, treat it as a new sound. It may take a long time to proceed from one sound to the next and it is possible that you will need several months of daily practice.

Warning:

If after some time you begin to hear sounds during the day, do not continue with this technique. Although it is not a matter of hallucination it could interfere with your working life without providing you with any particular benefits. A very advanced Nada-Yogi is capable of hearing voices even when entirely awake, but certain essential preparations, not mentioned here, must have been made with the guide of a Guru. To hear the voice of the unknown belongs to the Siddhis (supernatural powers). One particular Indian sect, called Kanapishachi (spirit in the ear), is often consulted by people seeking advice. They sound a bell next to their ear until they hear a voice which will answer the question. This practice leads to deafness after a time and Kanapishachis do not hear well.

Chapter 9*

Antar-Mauna

Although we are not conscious of it there is a constant stream of thoughts, emotions, impressions and sensations flowing through us. We are incapable of following it, even when we are trying very hard. Only when we reverse the process, trying to achieve inner peace, do we discover these incessent inner activities.

It is easy to achieve general physical and mental relaxation, particularly if Pranayama is included in one's practices; this relaxation does not always last and one longs for a method which will help to keep this state permanently. The goal is reached when one becomes both observer and witness of all one's activities. When this stage has been reached the witnessing does not only concern awareness in the waking state but also the knowledge that one is sleeping or dreaming. At the same time it also includes detachment from the process of thinking. The discovery is soon made that one does not think oneself but that 'it' is thinking within one. This is easy to understand when we realize that eight to nine parts of our brain are working unconsciously while the other areas are not developed. In other words, our lives are directed from realms over which we have no control. To give an example: Most of our opinions are nothing but reflections of associations formed by certain cerebral patterns.

The danger consists in the identifications with thoughts and actions, as we believe that these phenomena derive from our innermost being. There are two possibilities of escaping this dilemma: one is to develop most of the brain with the help of the secret techniques of Kriya-Yoga (see chapter 10); the second one is to achieve inner tranquillity, the stage in which the source of thoughts, pictures, desires, etc. becomes clear. This develops the capacity to discard these or to replace them with others.

It is stated that a sage or a saint is pure; he has no 'bad' thoughts and therefore he is 'good'. This is nonsense. Christ as well as many saints (for instance St Anthony) have been tempted, but they realized, out of their inner tranquillity, that neither temptations nor bad thoughts were fundamental parts of their personality. Bad thoughts and temptations lose their importance and effectiveness when watched with detachment. They are like fireworks in the sky which fade away. It is wrong to suppress negative thoughts. When, for instance, one wishes to get rid of an unpleasant neighbour or to seduce one's brother's wife, those desires are quickly inhibited and expelled. One only allows the 'good' elements to emerge, those which have been accepted by authority, education and society. The result is that the dross in the subconscious, instead of being removed, piles up until one either drowns in it or becomes paralysed; sometimes these Samskaras become exposed in chaotic eruption. The result can be a comparatively harmless neurosis or hallucinations leading to serious schizophrenia.

The inner silence is the final point of a process of sublimation, not of a process of selection. This silence is not simply tranquillity, but a tranquillity which has been achieved and mastered. The clarification of the subconscious can be reached with the technique of Antar-Mauna. In a sense, it can be practised incessantly, as it consists of watching and observing oneself while speaking, eating, walking, reading, etc. This is the secret of the peace and harmony of the masters. It is a constant natural stage, like the repetition of the Mantra in Japa-Yoga. Beside this there is an intensive method, consisting of six steps. Each step can only produce results if the preliminary stage has been mastered.

Techniques similar to Antar-Mauna can be found in the scriptures of various Vedic, Tantric and Buddhist schools. Most psychological systems in the West, dealing with similar problems, apply methods resembling Antar-Mauna. Yogic experiences have been analysed and compared with the knowledge of the West by various authorities, such as I. Sen, Mircea Eliade, H. Dumolan, M. Fryba, R. S. Mishra, I. Mumford, Ananda Bhavani, D. T. Suzuki, Evans-Wentz and others. The purely medical side of Yoga has often been examined in Eastern Europe and the USA but so far a comparison of therapeutic methods has not yet been tackled.

It would be interesting to compare Antar-Mauna with the self-analysis of Karel Horney, aiming at the integration of personality, or with the work of Erich Fromm directed at 'productive orientation'. In its last stages Antar-Mauna could be combined with C. G. Jung's *Active Imagination.* At first, Antar-Mauna has many similarities with the *Autogenic Training* by J. H. Schultz, *Fractionized Active Hypnosis* by E. Kretschmer, *Progressive Relaxation* by E. Jacobson, *Psychosynthesis* by R. Assagioli, *Relaxation-Activation-Training* by M. Machac. Practically speaking, these techniques contain certain parts of Yoga-Nidra (see chapter 7). Until recently it was impossible to do any serious research into Yoga techniques, as these were kept secret and, whatever had been put down in writing was couched in symbolic, allegorical language understandable only to the advanced Yogi. Another disadvantage was the superficial translations of these scriptures, which not only lost part of the meaning, but also misled the seeker.

In 1932, J. H. Schultz in his *Autogenic Training* compared this with Yoga, although he himself had neither known all the essential facts, nor did he evaluate them correctly. To him the path with seven steps leading to realization, as explained in the concept of the Cakras, was nothing but a compressed eight-fold path in the sense of Patanjali. He does not seem to have recognized or accepted the importance of the Cakras. Furthermore, he mistakes the Kriyas of Hatha-Yoga (various purifying and other actions) with the powerful Kriya-Yoga. Another of his errors was that he presumed that the induced sensations of hot or cold with their vasomotor changes are excluded from Yoga—yet they play an important part in Yoga-Nidra.

It has to be stressed that there are various symptoms connected with thresholds dividing one stage from the next; before these have been clearly experienced and evaluated, no further step must be taken.

The six stages:

1. *Observation and awareness of sense-perceptions* You should perceive all sounds in your surroundings simultaneously, that is avoid concentrating on a single sound or noise. When you are not distracted by sound or noise any more, you are ready to proceed to the second stage.

Note: Mastery of this stage can lead into Pratyahara, if all sense perceptions are integrated.

2. *Observation of spontaneously emerging thoughts, feelings, desires, etc* Be careful not to let slip even unpleasant or seemingly unimportant thought-splinters. It might happen that you realize afterwards that a fragment of thought did not register. Always keep your distance—not *you* are thinking but *it* is thinking inside you. When more and more thought forms emerge in frightening dimensions and you are in danger of being drowned by your overflowing subconscious, stop and advance to stage 3.

Note: Although it is the goal to clarify the subconscious, one cannot afford to allow more and more pictures to emerge. While psycho-analysis tries to solve the problems of the subconscious by projection, this practically infinite process is stopped in Antar-Mauna, as it is impossible to bring light to the whole subconscious.

3. *Observation and development of a single thought* This thought might concern an every day occurrence, for instance: 'I am hungry, I get up and go into the kitchen, I take a knife and cut off a piece of bread', etc. Follow this with details to the end and then dismiss the subject. Allow a vacuum of a score of seconds and tackle the next thought. You will be disturbed by spontaneously emerging thoughts which will become more and more insistent. If you are overwhelmed by too many thoughts advance to the next step.

Note: It is easier to do this process with negative thoughts. The change of thoughts is essential because brooding over a single thought is the root of neurosis. The more you advance in this analysis, the more resistance will surge up.

4. *Observation and instant dismissal of spontaneous thoughts* This is more difficult than it sounds. The constant effort of repelling thought forms, which one wishes to observe more clearly, is very strenuous.
5. *Inner void, Pratyahara* This threshold is the most dangerous, because one easily sinks into not-consciousness.

Note: This stage becomes more and more dangerous the more often one plunges into 'not-consciousness'. This is known as Jada Samadhi and in Yoga it is called the realm of Tamas (darkness). It can cause severe physical and mental disturbances.
6. *Awareness of sleep* Now you are asleep but realize that you are unconscious.

Note: In this as in number 5 there can be 'not-conscious' sleep (to be distinguished from normal sleep, in which one is unconscious). This 'not-conscious' sleep is called Laya-Samadhi and it can happen that the heart stops beating. It is most important that at the moment of this kind of sleep the symbol (Ishta Devata) emerges automatically and will be held incessantly.

The first technique ought to be practised between ten and twenty times, before beginning with the second. The second technique remains the same throughout; according to your own development certain parts will be more stressed than others. You will be under the impression that the remaining text becomes superfluous—it might even irritate or annoy you—but it must not be omitted as it becomes the checking point of your attention. This means that you have to listen to the whole text every time you use this meditation. In case of a lack of time use only the first technique.

TEXT

Technique 1

Sit or lie down, entirely relaxed, no tension anywhere.
Keep yourself open

Neither dislike nor like any kind of experience coming to you, do not react to whatever comes.

No reaction to pleasure, no reaction to thoughts, no reaction to emotions.

Allow the sense perceptions to run freely, perceive everything happening around you. Do not get disturbed but follow the disturbance, follow the thoughts, follow the sounds, follow emotions and observe in which way they disturb you.

Thoughts are either spontaneous or they are called up from the depth of your mind.

Mere thoughts or thoughts stimulated by inner or outer irritations.

Listen to all disturbing sounds and follow them with uttermost concentration into every detail. Listen to the sounds as a detached witness, as if you watched the whole from a corner of your brain.

I think...

I listen...

I feel...

Think, listen, feel, again and again, watch the process of your awareness.

Thoughts will emerge without rhyme or reason—unwanted—from the dark depth of your past.

Senseless, meaningless, flaring up, a glimmer in your eyes.

You...

you must be quick and attentive, otherwise it will be impossible to follow the whizzing forms of your consciousness.

You will follow the free stream of your consciousness,
naturally, willingly or unwillingly.

Sometimes everything will stop, it becomes dark and you cannot see anything.

Nothing emerges.

When the consciousness cannot find a form, it slides away.

Nevertheless, 'it' is thinking inside you, even now you are thinking, although you cannot see it. A veil has been drawn.

Tear it away and again—

look at all your thoughts.

They belong to past and present, a summer lightning with various associations.

When a thought emerges, look at it, register it and then let it go.

Many thoughts come which you do not like; you do not wish to notice them and you will try to turn away. This is quite natural; to escape from our own thoughts is our normal mental attitude. Both our memory and our past are inhibited. When the veil has been removed, the forms can be seen and when everything is free one is filled with happiness. When the past appears be a detached witness, you will then be free from all tensions and dullness.—The most important thing is:

SEE YOURSELF:

First: become free

Second: see yourself, the whole process,
be relaxed and watch it.

Do not resist your thoughts,
Do not tarry,
Do not suffer from guilt,
Think freely, watch everything, don't miss anything.
You are not these thoughts, but you are their witness.
Totally detached.
Try it. Continue on the same line. Do not be biased.

Keep away from everything, be the witness of your thoughts, be the witness of experiences. You are not these thoughts, you are not an enemy of your mind. You are quite indifferent, you neither hate nor love.

You do not see yourself thinking. It is difficult to see oneself thinking; though it is very easy to think unconsciously, it is difficult to think consciously as the process of thinking is automatic. Sometimes this process is caused through outer influences.

Spontaneous thoughts come from the depth of your personality. Remove the veil covering your inhibitions so that they can emerge spontaneously.

But when they do not arise by themselves we have to stimulate the process.

When consciousness can unfold freely, that is, when the veil covering your tensions has been partly or wholly removed, you will be faced with horrifying images. Good and beautiful thoughts will come later: should they arise now, it would be self-deceit; these kinds of thoughts are rooted in your social behaviour, in your surroundings, because you know that they are expected from you and because you believe that you have to be good and kind and honourable, etc.

But this is not the *real* manifestation of your consciousness. It is the negative side of your consciousness, of your personality and of your past.

It *has* to come out—and if not in thoughts it will come out in actions.

Do not be shy nor be paralysed.

Remain a witness of the whole process. Do not try to interpret nor evaluate your thoughts, do not identify yourself with them.

Remain a detached witness.

It may be tiredness, or sleepiness or a thought from outside or a noise; repeat to yourself: 'I am a witness of what I hear, of the thoughts or desires which pass by, and I am practising Antar Mauna.'

Tell yourself: 'I am watching my thoughts, even if they are stupid.'

Watch even the most idiotic thoughts.

Uninterrupted awareness.

Untiring awareness of thoughts, noticing everything, both what happens inside and outside you.

Your inner consciousness is the witness.

Your inner consciousness is the witness.

The nearer you draw to this inner consciousness, the better you will be able to watch.

If you awaken your inner consciousness in the form of a witness there will be nothing that escapes you.
Even a blinking of your eyes or a trembling of your body, the most silent thought, everything
everything will be registered.
If you are able to keep the inner consciousness awake, everything which concerns you or which happens in you will be noticed.
No thought
No emotion
conscious, subconscious, unconscious
will be revealed to you. Your whole personality will unfold before you.

The two most important things are:

1. Keep your inner consciousness incessantly awake.
2. Allow everything to take shape and to flow naturally, undisturbed

Thoughts
Emotions
Sensations
Desires
Every process must be realized by the inner awareness.
Peace
Anger
Disturbances
Pleasant and unpleasant thoughts, inside and outside.
All dimensions of awareness must be watched.
Everything which can be understood, anything which is discernible and recognizable must be seen.

And when thoughts cease, register that nothing comes.
If something painful arises, recognize it. Your inner awareness is the witness.
Retain everything that you hear, see, know, feel.
I hear
I see
I know
I feel
All this will be a wonderful experience, a clearance of the inner cess-pool, a purification and a self-analysis.
Free mind and alertness.
Continue, freely and thoroughly.
Freedom of thought and awareness.
Open your subconscious, go on searching;

(*2 minute pause*)

Slowly come back, leave your thoughts and subconscious, because Antar Mauna is over. Open your eyes.

Technique 2

HARI OM HARI OM HARI OM

Sit in a comfortable posture. No more movement
Close your eyes.
No more movement
Absolutely motionless.
Realize your surroundings, be aware of your surroundings.

Notice your surroundings.
Open yourself to every experience.
Do not try to control your mind.
Do not go inside
Do not go inside but sense the external.
Keep open and receive everything that happens inside and outside this room.
Develop constant awareness of the external.
Listen to every sound Listen to every sound
Keep your mind open Keep your mind open
Your sense organs receive everything from outside, let them be antennae in the space surrounding you.
Absorb all outer experiences outer perceptions
Develop constant awareness for all things in this room, the instructions, the noises from outside. Be like radar for cosmic perceptions. Catch even the most unimportant sounds from outside, feel what is happening around, listen to all sounds simultaneously.
Do not go inside—do not stay inside—do not close your awareness.
Let your awareness flow, flow evenly outside in all directions.
Grasp every sound, sense everything, everything around you.
Let your awareness stretch out, strain it suddenly in the direction from where you have perceived something. Follow every sound.
Keep yourself open.
Your awareness must be free, your awareness must flow everywhere.
Do not remain in yourself, sense in all directions.
Do not resist disturbing sounds, enter them, allow them to affect you. Let the outer world flow into you and allow your awareness to flow in all directions. Be like an aerial. Receive everything. No thoughts, only awareness of your surroundings.
Develop your capacity of sensing This is neither concentration nor meditation. It is the development of sensing to its uttermost. Go as far as your awareness can go.

Grasp even the smallest sound in the atmosphere and feel everything that is happening in this room and outside, here inside and outside at the same time.

When two sounds become audible somewhere outside, you ought to be capable to absorb them simultaneously.

You should accept all noises with your consciousness, nothing should escape you.

Conscious awareness of the surroundings.

Conscious awareness of the surroundings.

Be like a burning lamp, radiating light in all directions.

In the same way allow your consciousness to radiate in all directions.

This is called *even* awareness.

Not a conditioned awareness   not only a simple awareness

Neither a concentrated awareness nor a focused awareness, but an *even* awareness.

Develop an even awareness   not a partial awareness

When you hear a car pass outside, do not concentrate on the sound as, if you concentrate on it, you will miss hearing the voice.

Listen   listen

Do not concentrate

Please understand it

Radiate your awareness   Radiate your awareness,

to illuminate every perception

Develop this capacity   develop this talent

Even awareness of your surroundings

Even awareness of your surroundings

The awareness of all sensations, as far as you can penetrate

with your awareness.

Concentrate on Cidakasa

no movement please.

Concentrate on Cidakasa

Concentrate on Cidakasa
Concentrate on Cidakasa and develop awareness of your thoughts
Do not control your thoughts
Do not control your thoughts
Do not control your thoughts
Do not think
But develop the conscious awareness of all spontaneous thoughts.
But develop the conscious awareness of all spontaneous thoughts
Which emerge in your Cidakasa.
Be a witness of your spontaneous thoughts
Be a witness of your spontaneous thoughts
Do not think
Do not control your thoughts
Do not think
Do not control your thoughts
Concentrate on Cidakasa and look out for thoughts
Do not control your thoughts
Do not allow even a single thought to escape
Do not allow even a single thought to escape
Do not think
Watch spontaneous thoughts

(*1 minute pause*)

Relax your mind and watch your thoughts
Relax your mind and watch your thoughts
Relax your mind and watch your thoughts
Concentration on Cidakasa
What am I thinking? What am I thinking? What am I thinking?

Put the question as follows:
What am I thinking, what did I think?

(*1 minute pause*)

What am I thinking, what did I think?
What shall I think?

(*quarter-minute pause*)

What am I thinking?

(*quarter-minute pause*)

What did I think?

(*quarter-minute pause*)

What do I wish to think?

(*quarter-minute pause*)

Relax your mind and watch your spontaneous thoughts

(*1 minute pause*)

Develop spontaneous awareness of spontaneous thoughts.
It does not matter in the least, if, in between, you feel you have lost the thread. After some time ask once more:
'What did I think?' Then cogitate on what you did think.
Sometimes you will be so overburdened with thoughts that you do not know what you were thinking, but as soon as you come back ask yourself: 'What did I think?'
Concentration on Cidakasa
Concentration on Cidakasa
Concentration on Cidakasa

Choose a thought and think it over.
Choose a subject which is dear to you and think about it for some time until I say 'Stop'.
Think about a subject for some time until I say 'Stop'.
Do not play about with spontaneously emerging thoughts.
Do not play about with spontaneous thoughts, but choose one thought according to your wish.
Imagine one thought and develop its theme systematically until I say 'Stop'.

(*half a minute pause*)

Concentration on Cidakasa
Stop   No thinking   no thinking   no thinking
No thinking   Look into your Cidakasa
No thinking   Look into your Cidakasa
No thinking   just looking into the inner space.
And again a thought, but a new one, a different one, out of your own choice, not one which emerges by itself.
Develop this thought for a while

(*1 minute pause*)

Stop   Concentration on Cidakasa and no thinking
No thinking   No thinking   No thinking
Concentration on Cidakasa
Develop another thought of your choice and follow it systematically and with greatest concentration.

(*half a minute pause*)

Stop   No thinking
Concentration on Cidakasa and   No thinking   no thinking

Concentration on Cidakasa No thinking
Concentration on your body, concentration on your physical body.
Complete awareness of the whole physical body until the body becomes a field of force, an energetic block.
Uninterrupted, unceasing, entire awareness of the whole body.
Awareness of tranquillity, awareness of immobility, awareness of compactness.
Not even the slightest vibration in any part of the body.
Even sensing of the body.
Concentration on the breath in the nostrils.
Concentration on the breath in the nose
Concentration on the breath in the nose.

The breath ascends to the centre of the eyebrows and descends, flowing through the nose and two inches outside. Imagine these points and feel your breath ascending and descending between them and Bhrumadya. Concentrate on this slight breath ascending and descending between these two points. Concentrate on this fine breath, which is abstract, and add the suggestion: 'No thinking'. Join the breath with the suggestion 'No thinking'.

From Bhrumadya to the end of the nostrils and two inches outside.
Concentration on the flow of the breath with the suggestion not to think.
Even, uninterrupted awareness.
This breath is quite near and natural.
Bring your consciousness nearer to this breath, fuse it.
Bring the concentration and consciousness of the breath together.
Join the breath with your concentration.

Let them become one so that they flow together through your nose.
Suggestion: 'No thinking'.
Join your awareness with the breath.

They are the same.

Bring your consciousness nearer to this breath. And let them flow together through your nose and two inches outside.

No thinking.

(*half a minute pause*)

Concentration on Cidakasa, the breath in the nose and the suggestion: 'No thinking'.

Visualize Cidakasa with the breath in your nose and the suggestion 'No thinking'.

Now take yourself outside, sense your surroundings. Turn outside and feel what goes on around you.

Open yourself entirely

(*half a minute pause*)

Please turn outside, open yourself to the outside.

Let your consciousness stream outside.

Develop even awareness of your surroundings.

Do not control yourself   Do not switch off

Keep yourself open to everything around you.

Concentration on Cidakasa, the breath and not thinking.

Concentration on the breath and no thinking and on Cidakasa

Constant awareness of the breath.

Constant awareness of the breath flowing through the nose and not thinking.

Constant suggestion not to think and awareness of Cidakasa.

(*three-quarter-minute pause*)

Now turn outside, towards your surroundings and feel it quickly.

Be quick

Turn outside

Turn inside

Inside means: Cidakasa, breath through the nose and no thinking.
Outside means: sense your surroundings.
Turn inside quickly

(quarter-minute pause)

Outside

(quarter-minute pause)

Inside

(quarter-minute pause)

Outside

(quarter-minute pause)

Inside

(quarter-minute pause)

Outside and be quick, very quick

(quarter-minute pause)

Inside

(quarter-minute pause)

Outside

(quarter-minute pause)

Inside

(quarter-minute pause)

Outside

(quarter-minute pause)

Yet more outside, still more, still more outside
Inside, more, deeper, inside, inside

(half a minute pause)

Concentration on your awareness concentration on your awareness with which you feel what you have done and what you are doing.
Concentration on 'I am'.
It is the same: concentration on your awareness and concentration on 'I am'.

(*1 minute pause*)

Relax your body
Relax your mind

Open your eyes

HARI OM TAT SAT

Chapter 10

Ajapa-Japa

When, with the help of Hatha Yoga and the techniques described in this book, one has become able to experience the whole body as a field of energy and the being has become centralized, when there are no more difficulties with relaxation, the time has come to direct consciousness inside the central nervous system. This can be done with the often quoted and, until now kept secret, teachings of Kriya Yoga. (Kriya means action.) It is impossible to teach this before the pupils have gone through a certain amount of preparation and fulfilled the conditions demanded. In Monghyr, only a few groups have so far been introduced to this most powerful of all techniques. The preparations included a special diet, many hours of daily practice, and silence for several weeks. The Kriya Yoga mentioned by Paramhansa Yogananda (*Autobiography of a Yogi*), which is taught in his centres in the USA, represents only a preliminary state. Through these 'actions' an enormous amount of heat is created, bursting open all suppressed areas in the subconscious and flooding consciousness, so that the strangest things can happen. Therefore it is necessary to work with a strong Guru who knows all the laws of mental phenomena and has mastered them. This is one of the main reasons for keeping Kriya Yoga a secret. When not controlled, it can be dangerous for the aspirant.

Generally speaking, Kriya Yoga consists of various practices which, taken singly, have only a fractional effect. They are mostly Mudras reinforced with certain movements of the consciousness in the body and co-ordinated with breath. Ajapa Japa plays a central, important part in this system, it is given here in a simplified form, which, nevertheless, produces powerful effects.

In preparation you must practise Pranayama for ten minutes, preferably alternate breathing and Bhastrika; afterwards you should sit in Padadirasana (this means that you sit in Vajrasana, the Japanese position, in which one sits on one's calfs: press the hands under the armpits, right hand under the left armpit and vice-versa). After some ten minutes both nostrils should be free. Shushumna, the central psychic channel in the spine, begins to course, creating a symmetry between Ida and Pingala, Moon and Sun. Both the autonomic and vegetative nervous system are in balance. Use your Mala for Ajapa–Japa. Mark the 13th and the 49th bead.

Technique

1. Sit upright and relax. Concentrate on your spine. Inhale in Ujjayi Pranayama and feel how the breath seems to fill the spine, beginning from the bottom (Muladhara Cakra) up to the top of the spine (near Ajna Cakra).

   Although it is clear that the air goes into the lungs, it is easier to co-ordinate the movement of consciousness in the spine with the breath; when you reach the top of the spine, ejaculate the syllable OM (not AUM but OOmmmm) with a very short O and a long, humming M. Together with the M, consciousness is gliding down the spine. If you reach the bottom before the breath (and the sound M) you must feel how the consciousness piles up there like a flow of honey, spiralling up and forming a small mound. Should you arrive later, then wait with the inhalation until you have forced your consciousness down. Then inhale again in Ujjayi and begin to rise.

   The whole process is repeated thirteen times. Start again at beginning of Mala.
2. Fold your tongue and press its underside against the palate. This is called Khechari-Mudra.

   (*a*) Inhale from Manipura Cakra (navel) to Vishuddhi Cakra (throat) and exhale from Vishuddhi to Manipura. If this process of imagination comes to you easily, replace it by:

(*b*) Inhale and exhale between Muladhara and Ajna Cakra.
Repeat this forty-nine times.

3. Like number 2, but listen to the breath, which in inhalation sounds like SO, and in exhalation like HAM. Do not pronounce these syllables mentally but listen to their sound.
Repeat this fifty-nine times.
4. Like 3, but with the difference that you co-ordinate SO with inhalation and HAM with exhalation. This time begin with the exhalation HAM, followed by the inhalation SO.
In 3 it was SOHAM SOHAM etc. Now it is HAMSO HAMSO etc.
Repeat fifty-nine times.
5. Up to here it is permitted to change your position, but from now onwards, you must remain motionless.
Do not concentrate on your breath, but listen only to the SO'HAM. From now onwards the awareness of SOHAM HAMSO is following a constant circulation in the spine.

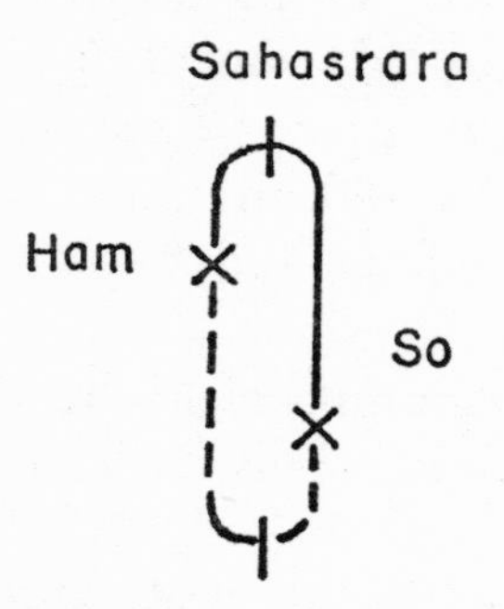

Beginning in Muladhara with SO, let this rise up to your head, that is, not only to Ajna but to the top of the head, and continue with SO for a short stretch, although you start exhaling when SO has reached the crown of the head. Change over to HAM without interruption and continue again for a short stretch while you have started the inhalation, then change without interruption to SO. The 'trick' consists in bridging the two gaps between inhalation and exhalation (see diagram). The result is a continuous circulation which, if you succeed without pause, leads directly into Pratyahara.

The whole movement takes place in the spine with SO behind and HAM in front of it.

6. After Pratyahara, concentrate on the brain, visualizing this in the shape of a room with four walls, ceiling and floor. Grope along this room from inside with your awareness: Forehead, right temple, back of the head, left temple, ceiling, floor. There, at the back of the head, is an opening in the floor leading to Sushumna.
7. Concentrate on your Ishta devata or your chosen symbol in Bhrumadhya.

Note: The ten most important techniques described in this book are taught by Swami Satyananda at the Bihar School of Yoga in Monghyr. There are yet other methods which can only be taught at a school or with a teacher after the student has absorbed some principal concepts and is thoroughly familiar with the cakras. However many different kinds of meditation have been studied, each person will find that he can enter the inner labyrinth (after having removed the first barriers) by using *one* method which corresponds with his own structure and which enables him to reach the final goal. To those who have reached it, all methods are equal.

Those, for whom this book is sufficient, will, corresponding with a magnificent law, find a master who will guide them and help them to advance on their path. Others might finally discover the Guru in themselves. The master of masters, the Mahayogin, dwells in each of us as the root of life and the source of consciousness.